Series/Number 07–144

# POLYTOMOUS ITEM RESPONSE THEORY MODELS

**REMO OSTINI**
*University of Queensland*

**MICHAEL L. NERING**
*Measured Progress*

**SAGE PUBLICATIONS**
*International Educational and Professional Publisher*
Thousand Oaks   London   New Delhi

*For information:*

Sage Publications, Inc.
2455 Teller Road
Thousand Oaks, California 91320
E-mail: order@sagepub.com

Sage Publications Ltd.
1 Oliver's Yard
55 City Road
London EC1Y 1SP
United Kingdom

Sage Publications India Pvt. Ltd.
B-42, Panchsheel Enclave
Post Box 4109
New Delhi 110 017  India

Printed in the United States of America.

*Library of Congress Cataloging-in-Publication Data*

Ostini, Remo.
Polytomous item response theory models / Remo Ostini, Michael L. Nering.
    p. cm. — (Quantitative applications in the social sciences; 07-144)
Includes bibliographical references and index.
ISBN 0-7619-3068-X (pbk.)
    1. Social sciences—Mathematical models. 2. Item response theory.
3. Psychometrics. 4. Social sciences—Statistical methods. I. Nering, Michael L.
II. Title. III. Series: Sage university papers series. Quantitative applications in the
social sciences; no. 07-144.
H61.25.O86 2006
150′.287—dc22

                                                    2005005274
This book is printed on acid-free paper.

05   06   07   08   09   10   9   8   7   6   5   4   3   2   1

| | |
|---|---|
| *Acquisitions Editor:* | Lisa Cuevas Shaw |
| *Editorial Assistant:* | Karen Gia Wong |
| *Production Editor:* | Melanie Birdsall |
| *Typesetter:* | C&M Digitals (P) Ltd. |
| *Proofreader:* | Tracy Marcynzsyn |
| *Indexer:* | Naomi Linzer |

# CONTENTS

# SERIES EDITOR'S INTRODUCTION

When students take aptitude tests or when respondents answer attitudinal survey questions, the purpose of the test or questionnaire is to assess certain aptitude or attitude by asking test or survey questions. In reality, test or observed scores $x_i$ are recorded with measurement error $e_i$. According to Classical Test Theory (CTT),

$$\chi_i = \tau_i + e_i,$$

where $\tau_i$ is the true (or latent) score that cannot be observed directly. One of the limitations of CTT applications is their test dependency for both test difficulty and test discrimination. For example, test difficulty directly affects the observed test scores. Higher "aptitude" scores are associated with tests composed of easier items, and vice versa. Enter Item Response Theory (IRT). IRT has several advantages over CTT. Whereas CTT item statistics depend fundamentally on the subset of items and persons examined, IRT item and person parameters are invariant, thus allowing the researcher to assess the contribution of individual items as they are added or omitted from a test. Moreover, the IRT model can distinguish item bias from true differences on the attribute or aptitude measured, whereas the CTT model cannot. This makes it possible to conduct rigorous tests of measurement equivalence across experimental groups, which is particularly useful when conducting research in cross-cultural settings where mean differences on the attribute or aptitude being measured are expected.

The basic IRT model for binary response variables may have up to three parameters and can take the logistic form of

$$P_{ij}(\theta_i) = c_j + (1 - c_j)\frac{e^{a_j(\theta_i - b_j)}}{1 + e^{a_j(\theta_i - b_j)}},$$

where $P_{ij}(\theta_i)$ is the probability that a given student $i$ with ability $\theta_i$ answers a random item $j$ (or $x_j$) correctly (or $P_{ij}[x_j = 1]$ for binary data), $a_j$ is the item discrimination, $b_j$ is the item difficulty, and $c_j$ is the pseudo-guessing parameter. The common two-parameter IRT model is obtained when $c_j = 0$, and the one-parameter IRT model is obtained when $c_j = 0$ and $a_j = 1$.

More generally, the analysis of the relation between latent continuous variables and observed categorical variables—which can be binary or (ordered) polytomous—is known as Latent Trait Analysis (LTA). In psychometrics and educational testing, LTA is called IRT, whereas in the other social sciences, LTA is the better known term. There is so much overlap between the two that the terms often are used interchangeably.

There are two main variants of the LTA or IRT models. One is the Gaussian or normal-ogive model and the other is the popular logistic-ogive and Rasch-type model. The original Rasch model, attributed to the late Danish statistician Georg Rasch and introduced by Andrich in Monograph No. 68 in the QASS series, is a logistic-ogive LTA model for dichotomous data. The current title by Ostini and Nering extends the coverage to the situation where polytomous items constitute the data. My predecessor, Michael Lewis-Beck, who must have seen the need for covering the topic and to whom we should all be thankful, oversaw the first half of the editing. This book deals with many logistic-ogive variants of IRT for (ordered and unordered) polytomous data, including the nominal response model, the polytomous Rasch-type model such as the partial credit and the rating scale models, and the Samejima model, which is built on the cumulative boundary response function approach of Thurstone. No doubt, the book should help the diffusion of IRT in the social sciences.

— *Tim Futing Liao*
Series Editor

# ACKNOWLEDGMENTS

The authors would like to thank Jennifer Ostini and Liz Burton for their careful review of earlier drafts of this monograph. We would also like to thank Wonsuk Kim for his assistance in analysis and the editors of the QASS series for their valuable suggestions.

# POLYTOMOUS ITEM RESPONSE THEORY MODELS

REMO OSTINI
*University of Queensland*

MICHAEL L. NERING
*Measured Progress*

## 1. INTRODUCTION

### Measurement Theory

Mathematical models are very useful tools in the process of human enquiry. It can be argued that their use is what has driven the engine of science for the past century and has made it such a successful enterprise (Wright, 1997). Bartholomew (1987) suggests that a mathematical model elucidates the conceptual grounding and explicates the framework for a project, and in doing so, provides a context from which to conduct analyses and interpret results. Note that here and in the remainder of the text, we use the term *mathematical model* in its broadest sense and not, as it is sometimes used, as a proxy for deterministic models.

At a basic level, mathematical models can provide a means to quantify phenomena of interest. The process of counting objects involves the use of a relatively simple and direct mathematical model. Simple counts play a large role in the social sciences, but the usefulness of this approach is less certain here than in areas such as commerce and engineering. For example, Thorndike (1904) noted the difficulty of measuring as simple a skill as spelling, because spelling proficiency depends not only on how many words a person can spell (simple count) but also on how difficult those words are to spell.

Problems with simple mathematical models in the social sciences have led to the development of more appropriate models. In psychology, one of the earliest formalizations of a measurement theory for mental tests (Cattell, 1890), or psychological phenomena generally, is a set of mathematical models that has come to be called classical test theory (CTT). CTT derives from the pioneering work of Spearman (1904) and is built on measurement concepts borrowed from the physical sciences (Mislevy, 1996; also see Nichols, 1998). One of the central concepts that CTT has borrowed

1

from measurement in the physical sciences is the idea of errors in measurement. Indeed, it is partly because there are potentially large errors in psychological measurement that test theories are required (Lord & Novick, 1968). Measurement theory is also needed because the phenomena that psychologists study (e.g., traits) are not themselves directly measurable and must be studied indirectly through the measurement of other observable phenomena (Lord & Novick, 1968).

Ultimately, difficulties with testing the assumptions of CTT and applying the resulting model in practice have led to the development of alternative measurement models. These models are essentially extensions and liberalizations of the classical theory (Brennan, 1998).

## Item Response Theory

Item Response Theory (IRT) is an extension of CTT with mathematical roots that run deep in psychology, in the work of Fechner in the 1860s (Baker, 1992) and in Thurstone's (1925) early work (Bock, 1997a; Weiss, 1983). In IRT, these mathematical roots form an item-based test theory that itself has roots in the psychological measurement work of Binet, Simon, and Terman as far back as 1916 (Baker, 1992; Bock, 1997a). The formal basis of IRT as an item-based test theory is generally attributed to the work of Lawley (1943; see Baker, 1992; Weiss, 1983). His pioneering work was, in turn, expanded significantly by Lord (1952), who also formalized IRT's role as an extension of the classical theory (Baker, 1992). Subsequent work by Lord (1980; Lord & Novick, 1968) and Birnbaum (1968) has been instrumental in establishing an understanding and acceptance of IRT among psychological measurement practitioners. The Danish mathematician Rasch (1960, 1966, 1977) played a similarly influential role by developing separately a specific class of IRT models and showing that it had a number of highly desirable features.

General treatments of IRT can be found in Hambleton and Swaminathan (1985) and Andrich (1988b). The mathematical foundation of IRT is a function that relates the probability of a person responding to an item in a specific manner to the standing of that person on the trait that the item is measuring. In other words, the function describes, in probabilistic terms, how a person with a higher standing on a trait (i.e., more of the trait) is likely to provide a response in a different response category to a person with a low standing on the trait. This mathematical function has a prespecified form (usually a logistic ogive) and is now generally referred to as an item response function (IRF).

The main advantage of IRT is the fact that the item location ($b$) and the person trait level ($\theta$) are indexed on the same metric. Therefore, when a person's trait level is higher than the item location on the trait continuum, that person is more likely than not to provide a trait-indicating (positive, or true) response. The converse is true when a person's trait level is below the item location.

In typical discussion of dichotomous IRT models, the item category that represents a positive response (and is subsequently coded 1) is described as indicating a "correct" response to an item (the alternative category, coded 0, indicates incorrect responses). Furthermore, the item location parameter $b$ is commonly referred to as the item difficulty parameter.

References to correct responses and item difficulties lose their common meaning in the context of tests that attempt to measure a respondent's typical performance rather than his or her maximum performance. Measures of typical performance (MTPs) include, for example, tests used in personality, attitude, and interest measurement—what might be called predilection measurement in contrast to aptitude measurement. Although the language that has built up around IRT has a common meaning that is out of place in typical performance measurement, the mathematical models that comprise IRT are quite neutral about their application to either maximum or typical performance measures.

**Applying the IRT Model**

The mechanics of IRT can be presented most easily in terms of a dichotomous model, that is, a model for items with only two response alternatives. Typically, such items require responses that are either correct or incorrect. They can also be personality-type measurement items with, for example, true or false response options. We noted earlier that the central feature of IRT is that it specifies a way to model the probability of a particular response to a test item with respect to a continuous, underlying trait. This is typically accomplished by means of a monotonic function—the IRF.

The IRF shown in Figure 1.1 is a function that reflects the probability of selecting a positive (correct or keyed) response to an item. It can be thought of more generally as reflecting the probability associated with moving from one response category to the next along the entire trait continuum. In other words, the function depicts the probability of making the transition from responding in one category to responding in the next, across the boundary between categories that the ogival IRF represents.

When modeled by a logistic ogive, the IRF usually requires the estimation of two parameters. One is the location parameter, which describes where along the trait continuum the function is centered. The center of the function is defined as midway between its lower and upper asymptotes.

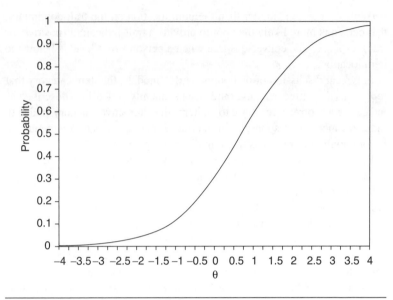

**Figure 1.1**     IRF for a Positive Response to a Dichotomous Item

More generally, the center of the function is at the point of inflection of the curve. The letter $b$ typically signifies the item's location parameter.

The item location parameter is modeled in the same metric as the parameter that describes a person's trait level. As a result, it also represents the amount of the trait being measured that is required for a person to be as likely to respond in the particular response category being modeled as to not respond in this category.

The second parameter that must be estimated to provide a description of an IRF is the parameter that indexes the slope of the function. This parameter, signified by the letter $a$, is usually estimated at the point of inflection of the function, which is also where the steepness of the slope is greatest. This parameter gives an indication of how well an item discriminates among people along the trait continuum. In other words, it shows how well an item can tell people apart with respect to the amount of a trait that they have. Another way of saying this is that highly discriminating items can tell with greater accuracy than poorly discriminating items whether people who have trait levels that are close together, and whose ability is close to the item's difficulty, are likely to provide different responses.

With these two parameters to describe the function, it is convenient to write the equation for the logistic form of an IRF as

$$P(\theta) = \frac{e^{a(\theta-b)}}{1 + e^{a(\theta-b)}}, \tag{1.1}$$

where $P(\theta)$ is shorthand for $P(x = i|\theta)$, and this, in turn, denotes the probability that the response to item $x$ is with option $i$ at a given trait level ($\theta$). In this case, response option $i$ refers to the positive item response option (i.e., more of the trait; a correct answer when there are only two options). With the dichotomous model, the equation for the function that describes the probability of responding in the alternative category (less of a trait; wrong answer) is simply 1 minus the right-hand side of Equation 1.1.

Typically, only the response function for one response category is modeled explicitly because the functions for each category are the complement of one another. Usually, only the positive category is modeled, with a monotonically increasing function (Figure 1.1). The complementary nature of the category functions means that knowing the characteristics of one function tells you all you need to know about the other function.

However, measurement items with multiple response options also exist, and their use is becoming more prevalent. Such items include rating scale items, such as the ubiquitous Likert-type items, as well as ability test items that provide partial credit for partially correct answers, portfolio assessment test formats, and even multiple-choice items when each response option is scored separately.

Polytomous IRT models for such items operate quite differently from dichotomous models. In these cases, knowledge of the characteristics of one of the response category functions does not determine the characteristics of the other category functions, and each category function therefore must be modeled explicitly. A corollary of the nondeterminate nature of the category response functions is that they are no longer exclusively monotonic functions. In the case of items with ordered categories, only the functions for the extreme negative and positive categories are monotonically decreasing and increasing respectively. Figure 1.2 shows that the function for the second category rises as the probability of responding in the most negative category decreases, but only up to a point, at which time it decreases as the probability of responding in the next category increases. Ultimately, the "next category" is the extreme positive category, which has a monotonically increasing function.

Inasmuch as the application of IRT is an exercise in curve fitting, the presence of nonmonotonic functions presents special problems. Such functions can no longer be described simply in terms of a location and a slope

6

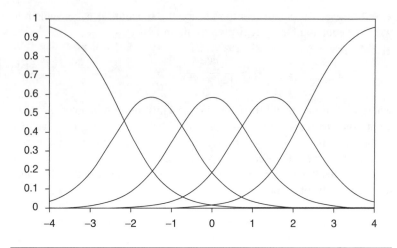

**Figure 1.2**    Response Functions for a Five-Category Polytomous Item

parameter. Actually selecting the appropriate mathematical form and subsequently estimating parameters for such unimodal functions is a significant challenge. Fortunately, in the case of ordered polytomous items, a solution to this problem has been found by treating polytomous items essentially as concatenated dichotomous items. Multiple dichotomizations of item response data are combined in various ways to arrive at appropriate response functions for each item category. The different ways in which the initial dichotomizations can be made and the different approaches to combining dichotomizations result in a variety of possible polytomous IRT models. In addition, different types of polytomous items require, or allow, different features to be incorporated into an applicable IRT model. The result is a range of possible polytomous models that far outstrips the number of available dichotomous models. Before addressing these issues in detail, a brief discussion will be provided to suggest why the extra complexity involved in modeling polytomous items might be justified.

## Reasons for Using Polytomous IRT Models

Perhaps the simplest and most obvious reason for the development of polytomous IRT models is the fact that polytomous items exist and are commonly used in applied psychological measurement. To be a comprehensive measurement approach, IRT must provide appropriate methods for modeling these data. The need for polytomous response formats may be most acute in the measurement of personality and social variables. Kamakura and

Balasubramanian (1989) suggest that dichotomous distinctions are often less clear in this context than in ability measurement settings and that "more subtle nuances of agreement/disagreement" (p. 514) are needed than dichotomous items permit. Similarly, Cox (1980) notes that items with two or three response alternatives are inadequate in this context because they cannot transmit much information and they frustrate respondents.

The existence of polytomous data also has consequences for statistical data analysis. Wainer (1982) points out that responses to polytomous items can be thought of as data distributions with short tails. This may affect statistical procedures, such as obtaining least squares estimators, which rely on assumptions of a Gaussian distribution. Rather than simply proceeding as though the data met the assumptions, a better approach, according to Wainer, is to use procedures designed specifically for this type of data, especially relevant IRT models.

Prior to IRT, the two most common methods for dealing with polytomous data were Thurstone and Likert scaling. Thurstone scaling is similar to IRT in that it scales items on an underlying trait using a standardized scale (Thurstone, 1927a, 1927b, 1929, 1931). However, to achieve Thurstone scaling, one must either assume that the trait is normally distributed in the population of interest or select items so that this is the case (Thurstone, 1925, 1927a). Likert (1932) showed that a simple summated rating procedure produced results equal to or better than Thurstone's method. The simplicity of the approach meant that Likert scaling was soon widely adopted as the method of choice for rating data such as those used in attitude measures. However, Likert scaling assumes a linear relationship between the response probability and the underlying trait (Hulin, Drasgow, & Parsons, 1983). Neither the normality assumption of Thurstone scaling nor the linearity assumption of Likert scaling are particularly plausible.

Psychometric issues also exist that make polytomous items attractive in comparison to dichotomous items. At a general level, one such issue is that polytomous items measure across a wider range of the trait continuum than do dichotomous items. This occurs simply by virtue of the fact that polytomous items contain more response categories than do dichotomous items.

Strictly speaking, of course, all items, dichotomous and polytomous, measure across the entire range of the trait continuum, from negative to positive infinity. However, the amount of measurement information provided by an item is peaked above the trait scale location of that item and then drops, often precipitously, at higher and lower trait levels. Paradoxically, the more information that an item provides at its peak, the narrower the range of the trait continuum about which the item provides useful information. The advantage of polytomous items is that, by virtue of their greater number of response categories, they are able to provide more information over a wider range of the trait continuum than are dichotomous items.

Masters (1988c) and Bejar (1977) note that the entire purpose of using more than two categories per item is to try to obtain more information about the trait level of the people being measured so that more precise trait-level estimates can be obtained. Masters (1988a) also points out that more detailed diagnostic information about respondents and items can be obtained from polytomous test items.

Samejima (1975, 1979b) demonstrates the increase in statistical information that is available from a polytomous IRT model in comparison to a dichotomous model. Conversely, though in a different context, Cohen (1983) demonstrates that reducing continuous or multiple category data to the dichotomous level leads to a systematic loss of measurement information.

Finally, Kamakura and Balasubramanian (1989) note two practical benefits that follow from using the more informative polytomous items in the context of marketing research: (a) Testing time and cost are decreased, and (b) there will be a positive effect on respondent motivation to participate in the measurement if respondents are required to respond to fewer test items. However, these benefits are more likely to be obtained in any context using simple fixed measurement scales, such as rating scales. They are unlikely to apply in ability measurement settings, where the creation and scoring of polytomous items incurs greater time and financial costs.

**Polytomous IRT Models**

As mentioned in the previous section, the key to making ordered polytomous IRT models work in practical terms is dichotomization. At this point, for the sake of simplicity, we will concentrate the discussion on the case of polytomous models for items with ordered categories. Ordered polytomous items are simply those where the response categories have an explicit rank ordering with respect to the trait of interest. Likert-type attitude items and partial credit cognitive ability items are examples of ordered polytomous items. Responses to such items are also referred to as graded responses in the literature. Items on the Raven Progressive Matrices test and most multiple-choice test items are examples of items where the response options are not designed with an explicit ordering.

Polytomous items are categorical items in the same way as dichotomous items; they simply have more than two possible response categories. Categorical data can be described effectively in terms of the number of categories into which the data can be placed. Ordered categories are defined by boundaries or thresholds that separate the categories. Logically, there is always one less boundary than there are categories. Thus, for example, a dichotomous item requires only one category boundary to separate the two possible response categories. In the same manner, a 5-point Likert-type item requires four boundaries to separate the five possible response categories.

## Two Types of Probabilities

Compared to dichotomous models, the primary additional complication with polytomous IRT models is that the distinction between response categories and the boundaries that separate them reflects two different types of conditional probabilities: (a) the probability of responding in a given category, and (b) the probability of responding positively rather than negatively at a given boundary between two categories.

In the dichotomous case, the two probabilities amount to the same thing. That is, the probability of responding positively rather than negatively at the category boundary (modeled by the IRF) also represents the probability of responding in the positive category. When there are more than two categories, this is no longer the case because there is always at least one category that is defined by two boundaries. In that case, the probability of responding *in* such a category is determined by the characteristics of, at least, the two adjacent boundaries.

Measurement practitioners typically are most interested in the probability of responding in a given category, as this is the basis for determining respondents' levels of ability, trait, or attitude. However, we have already noted that the unimodal response functions for middle categories (Figure 1.2) are difficult to model mathematically. Therefore, most polytomous IRT models proceed by modeling each category boundary separately with a dichotomous model and then combining all the boundary information for an item in a formally specified manner. Applying a dichotomous model at each category boundary gives the probability of responding positively rather than negatively at the specific boundary— hence the need for explicitly ordered categories. Combining the dichotomous information from each boundary gives the probability of responding *in* each individual category.

Consider a specific item with five categories separated by four category boundaries. Determining the probability of responding positively rather than negatively at the first boundary will, at a minimum, involve the responses in Category 1 and Category 2. However, the responses in Category 2 will also be required for determining the probability of responding positively rather than negatively at the second boundary (the boundary between Category 2 and Category 3). Thus, the probability of actually responding *in* Category 2 is a combination of the probability of responding positively at the first

10

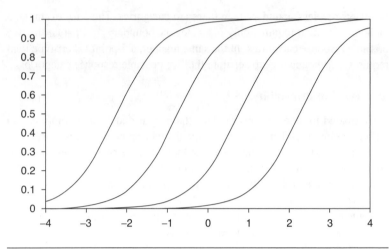

**Figure 1.3**    Category Boundary Response Functions for a Five-Category Polytomous Item

category boundary and the probability of responding negatively at the second category boundary.

Therefore, although the IRF of a dichotomous IRT model can represent the probability of responding on the positive side of the category boundary and also responding *in* the positive category, there is no single polytomous equivalent of the dichotomous IRF. The two kinds of probability simply cannot be represented in one type of polytomous response function. Instead, polytomous models require a specific function simply to represent the probability of responding at a category boundary. Because this particular function dichotomizes the response data at a category boundary, it has the typical ogive shape of the dichotomous IRF. Because it represents only the category boundary half of the response probability description represented by dichotomous IRFs, it will be referred to as the category boundary response function (CBRF). Examples of CBRFs are shown in Figure 1.3.

The other type of function that polytomous models require to represent the probability of responding *in* a given category was shown in Figure 1.2. In keeping with Chang and Mazzeo (1994) and Weiss and Yoes (1991), this type of function will be referred to as an item category response function (ICRF) to reflect its specific item category role. Unfortunately, researchers have used many different terms to refer to CBRFs and ICRFs. A selection of these is listed in the glossary.

## Two Types of Polytomous Models

There is also a distinction within both dichotomous and polytomous IRT models that is based primarily on the underlying measurement philosophy. The distinction is between Rasch-type models that attempt to conform to fundamental measurement theory and more pragmatically based models that do not. Conforming to fundamental measurement theory ultimately requires that IRT models adhere to the principle of specific objectivity. At the level of model parameters, specific objectivity requires that comparisons among item parameter values be independent of person parameter values and any other item parameters that are not being compared (and vice versa for person parameter comparisons). Rasch (1977) determined that for this to occur, the two types of parameters (item and person) in the measurement model must be additive and separable. This means that they must be in the form $(\theta - b)$ and cannot have a multiplicative form as in $a(\theta - b)$. Thus, although we mentioned earlier that estimation of a dichotomous IRF usually requires the estimation of two parameters, this is not true if adherence to the principle of specific objectivity is required. In that case, the discrimination ($a$) parameter must not be estimated. The dichotomous Rasch model therefore requires (allows) only the estimation of an item location parameter. At the parameter estimation level, specific objectivity is closely linked to the mathematical principle of sufficiency (Rasch, 1977), which provides the link between the measurement theory and the practical testing model in that it allows person and item parameters to be estimated independently (Wright, 1997).

In the polytomous arena, models that do not conform to fundamental measurement theory are direct successors to the Thurstone scaling approach (Thurstone, 1928a, 1928b, 1931, 1937; Edwards & Thurstone, 1952). They are also historical successors to equivalent models in the field of bioassay (Aitchison & Bennett, 1970; Aitchison & Silvey, 1957). Their IRT form, however, is largely due to a general framework developed by Samejima (1969, 1972, 1988).

## Category Boundaries

Two practical differences also present themselves when comparing Rasch and Thurstone/Samejima polytomous models. The first, perhaps obvious, difference is the mathematical form of the CBRF used to dichotomize the polytomous item data. Rasch models typically use a dichotomous Rasch model IRF to define category boundaries. Thurstone/Samejima models, on the other hand, typically use the 2-parameter logistic (2PL) model IRF to define category boundaries. As would be expected, the Rasch model choice of function is constrained by the additivity requirement of fundamental

12

measurement theory insofar as this theory forms the basis for the concept of specific objectivity (Wright, 1997). The second, less obvious, consequence of applying fundamental measurement theory to polytomous data is that the theory constrains the set of item category responses to which the dichotomization process is applied, and it does so in a particular manner. That is, it determines in a distinctive way which response data are used to define a Rasch CBRF.

As described earlier, a CBRF represents the probability of responding positively at a category boundary rather than responding negatively. However, in a polytomous item, there are at least two ways to respond positively rather than negatively. This is presented graphically in Figure 1.4.

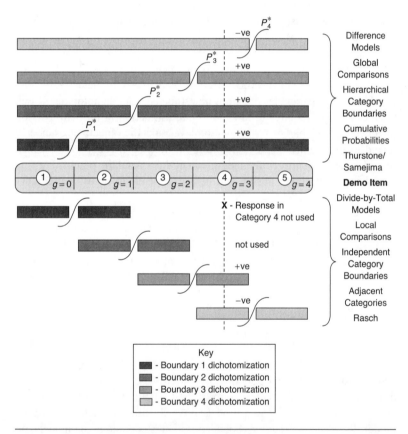

**Figure 1.4**    Graphical Representation of Two Approaches to Dichotomizing Polytomous Item Responses

Note: "−ve" denotes a negative response; "+ve" denotes a positive response.

Here it can be seen that "positively rather than negatively" can refer to just the two categories immediately adjacent to the category boundary (bottom half of Figure 1.4). Alternatively, the phrase can refer to all of the possible response categories for an item above and below the category boundary respectively (top half of Figure 1.4). There is also a third possibility. The phrase can also refer to a combination of the two alternatives just described. This leads to something of a hybrid polytomous model, which thus far has had little impact and therefore will not be discussed further here. Interested readers are referred to the work of Tutz (1990, 1997).

In order to maintain parameter separability and sufficient statistics for parameter estimation—that is, in order to maintain the theoretical and practical advantages of specific objectivity—Rasch-type polytomous models dichotomize polytomous data in the first manner just described (Molenaar, 1983; Wright & Masters, 1982). That is to say that the requirement for additive parameters means that Rasch model CBRFs dichotomously model responses only in categories immediately separated by a given boundary (Wright, 1997). As a result, the dichotomizations involve local comparisons and ignore the context of the responses in all other item categories. In contrast, Thurstone/Samejima models dichotomously model all possible response category responses above and below each category boundary respectively. These dichotomizations can be described as a set of global comparisons and directly incorporate the entire item category response context at each boundary. Thus, any given Rasch-model CBRF models responses in only two specific categories, whereas each Thurstone/ Samejima-model CBRF models the responses in every item category.

This is perhaps seen most easily by taking a specific response as an example. In Figure 1.4, a capital X is used to represent a response in Category 4 of the demonstration item. The vertical dashed line shows where this response would be counted in the category boundary dichotomization process, for each category boundary, in both the Rasch and the Thurstone/ Samejima approaches. The example shows that in the Thurstone/Samejima approach, this response would be used in estimating the category boundaries for all four of the boundaries separating the five response categories of this item. The response registers on the positive side of the first three category boundaries and as a response on the negative side of the boundary between Categories 4 and 5.

This approach is in marked contrast to the Rasch case. Because Rasch dichotomization involves only responses in categories adjacent to a specific boundary, the example response in Category 4 is directly relevant to modeling only two category boundaries. It registers as a positive response in the third category boundary dichotomization and as a negative response in modeling the fourth category boundary.

**Item Category Response Functions**

The two ways to model polytomous item category boundaries lead to two different ways of calculating ICRFs. Recall that the ICRFs provide the probability of responding *in* a particular category as a function of trait level (θ). Although details about the form and location of category boundaries is helpful, from a measurement, item analysis, and test construction perspective, it is the probability of responding in a category that is typically required. Because it is difficult to directly model this probability, it is obtained by combining information about category boundaries. How this information is combined naturally depends on how it is obtained initially.

*Thurstone/Samejima.* If $P_{i_g}$ is the probability of responding in a particular category (g) to item i and if $P_{i_g}^*$ represents a CBRF in the Thurstone/Samejima case (where both are conditional on θ), then

$$P_{i_g} = P_{i_g}^* - P_{i_{g+1}}^*. \tag{1.2}$$

That is, the probability of responding in a particular category is equal to the probability of responding above (on the positive side of) the lower boundary for the category $(i_g)$ minus the probability of responding above the category's upper boundary $(i_{g+1})$.[1] It can be seen that this gives the probability of responding between the category's two boundaries, which, intuitively and in fact, equals the probability of responding in the given category. Thus, for example, a response such as that in Figure 1.4, in the fourth category (i.e., g = 3) of a five-category item, would be represented algebraically as $P_{i_3} = P_{i_3}^* - P_{i_4}^*$.

This approach requires an additional definition for the probability of responding to an item at all (i.e., $P_{i_0}^*$), which is set to equal 1. Without this definition, it would not be possible to calculate the probability of responding in the first category. Similarly, the probability of responding above the highest category ($P_{i_5}^*$ in our example) is set to zero. This effectively states that the probability of responding in Category 5 of a five-category item is equal to the probability of responding positively at the fourth CBRF. More generally, the probability of responding in the highest category of an item with ordered categories is equal to the probability of responding positively at the highest CBRF. This type of polytomous model is referred to as a difference model by Thissen and Steinberg (1986).

All Thurstone/Samejima models take the form described in Equation 1.2. The various models within the family differ only in terms of how restrictions are applied to the parameters of the CBRFs, both within and across items. Specific restrictions and the different models that result from their implementation will be described in Chapter 4.

*Rasch.* The situation is somewhat different for Rasch models, largely because the dichotomization process involves the limited context of a local comparison. One result of this situation is that polytomous Rasch models rarely involve explicitly modeling category boundaries. Because these boundaries provide localized information, they are combined algebraically into a general expression for each ICRF. The expression that describes the probability of responding in a given item category takes the form

$$P_{i_g} = \frac{e^{z_{i_g}}}{\sum e^{z_{i_h}}}. \tag{1.3}$$

Here, $Z_{i_g}$ represents a sum of the differences between a given trait level and the location of each category boundary (i.e., $\sum(\theta - b_{i_g})$) up to the particular category $(g)$ in question. Seeing how this works in practice requires explicitly expanding out the equation for a specific example. If we again take the example from Figure 1.4, of a response in Category 4 $(g = 3)$ of a five-category item, then Equation 1.3 expands to show that the probability of this occurring is determined as

$$P_{i_3} = \frac{e^{(0)+(\theta-b_{i_1})+(\theta-b_{i_2})+(\theta-b_{i_3})}}{e^{(0)} + e^{(0)+(\theta-b_{i_1})} + e^{(0)+(\theta-b_{i_1})+(\theta-b_{i_2})} + e^{(0)+(\theta-b_{i_1})+(\theta-b_{i_2})+(\theta-b_{i_3})}}. \\ + e^{(0)+(\theta-b_{i_1})+(\theta-b_{i_2})+(\theta-b_{i_3})+(\theta-b_{i_4})}$$
$$\tag{1.4}$$

In a sense, the numerator describes the likelihood of someone at a given trait level responding in the positive category of each dichotomization up to the category in question. The denominator is the sum of the numerator values for every category in the item. It also ensures that the probability of responding in any single given category does not exceed 1, and that the accumulated probabilities of responding in a category, across all the categories for an item, sum to 1. The zero elements in the exponentials are (in this case) redundant in all of the exponential terms except the first term in the denominator. They are included here for completeness of exposition. Their function is to represent the possibility of a negative response at the first dichotomization, that is, failing to pass beyond the first CBRF location. In the denominator, the first exponent describes the requirement that a response must be made in one of the available categories even if it is only a negative response at the first category boundary. This probability is, of course, 1, showing that this element of the equation corresponds logically to the constraint in the Thurstone/Samejima case that $P^*_{i_0}$ equals 1. Given the form of the general expression for Rasch polytomous models shown in Equation 1.3, this type of model is described as a divide-by-total model by Thissen and Steinberg (1986). The major types of polytomous Rasch models, their relationships to each other, and variants of the major models are described in Chapter 3.

However, we will begin our description of specific models in Chapter 2 by looking at the most general of the models outlined in this book. It is a model that does not require items with ordered categories.

## 2. NOMINAL RESPONSE MODEL

The nominal response model (NRM) was introduced by Bock (1972) as a way to model responses to items with two or more nominal categories. A standard example of such an item is a multiple-choice item where the distractors are chosen with no particular order in mind in terms of the trait being measured. Clearly, there is explicit ordering with respect to the correct alternative in a multiple-choice item. This item category represents the highest category, in terms of the trait being measured, for the item. Baker (1992) notes that it is, in fact, rare to find items that are actually entirely nominally scored. Nevertheless, because the NRM can model nominally scored categories, it can be used to model responses to multiple-choice items or other items where any of the item categories are nominally scored. In doing so, it provides a way to solve a long-standing problem in educational measurement, that of simultaneously estimating all the parameters of a multiple-choice item's response alternatives (Baker, 1992).

The distinctive feature of this model, then, is that it can model unordered (nominal) data. The NRM is not built on the convenient concept of serial dichotomization resulting in category boundaries, which forms the basis of the graded models. Indeed, it cannot be, because ordered categories are required for category boundaries to be defined by this kind of dichotomization. Instead, the probability of responding in any given category is modeled directly, using an expression similar to that for polytomous Rasch models. Specifically, this is done by implementing a multivariate generalization of the logistic latent trait model (Bock, 1972).

Using the multivariate logistic function in the context of IRT is a specific application of a more general set of models developed by Bock to analyze qualitative data (Baker, 1992). Specifically, the NRM is an extension of multinomial, fixed-effects, logit-linear models to the mixed-effects setting of IRT (Bock, 1997b). The logit-linear models are, in turn, equivalent to the area in statistics known as loglinear models (Baker, 1992). Loglinear models are designed to investigate the interrelation of variables that form a contingency table (Dillon & Goldstein, 1984). Baker (1981) provides a detailed discussion of the specific orientations of the logit-linear and loglinear approaches.

**The Mathematical Model**

The mathematical definition of the multivariate logistic function provides a direct expression of $P_{i_g}$, the probability of responding in a particular item category, conditional on $\theta$:

$$P_{i_g} = \frac{e^{z_{i_g}}}{\sum_{h=1}^{m} e^{z_{i_h}}}, \tag{2.1}$$

where $h = 1, 2, \ldots, g, \ldots, m$. Also,

$$z_{i_h} = \zeta_{i_h} + \lambda_{i_h}\theta. \tag{2.2}$$

$Z_{i_h}$ is referred to as the multivariate logit. There is a vector of $m$ such logits for each item (Baker, 1992).

The quantities $\zeta_{i_h}$ and $\lambda_{i_h}$ are the item parameters for the $h$th category of item $i$. They have the usual interpretation for parameters in a linear equation. That is, $\lambda$ is the intercept parameter, and $\lambda$ is the slope parameter that relates $z_{i_h}$ to the latent trait ($\theta$). The intercept parameter reflects the overall popularity of alternative $h$ (Thissen, Steinberg, & Fitzpatrick, 1989). Attempts to estimate the values of the $\zeta$ and $\lambda$ parameters, however, encounter an identification problem (Baker, 1992). That is, the general function expressed in Equation 2.1 is invariant with respect to translation of the multivariate logit (Baker, 1992; Bock, 1972) and therefore must be anchored at some place. Bock (1972) chose to use the constraint that the sum of the multivariate logits within an item is zero. That is,

$$\sum z_{i_h} = 0, \tag{2.3}$$

which in turn implies that $\sum\zeta_{i_h} = 0$ and $\sum\lambda_{i_h} = 0$. An alternative method of constraining the parameters is to set the intercept and slope parameter of the first category being modeled for each item equal to zero. That is, $\zeta_{i_h} = \lambda_{i_h} = 0$ (Thissen, 1991). This method is used in the later example.

Although $\zeta$ and $\lambda$ are used to refer to the theoretical parameters of the nominal model, in practice, it is more common to represent the intercept and slope parameters by the letters $c$ and $a$, respectively. Note that here, the

$c$ parameter is not the same as is used in the dichotomous three-parameter logistic IRT model. In the NRM, it simply represents the intercept parameter of a linear equation.

An equivalent, linear form to Equation 2.2 for the dichotomous, normal ogive IRT model is provided by Baker (1992, Chapter 1). There, he shows that the transformations required to express the linear form of the equation in terms of the familiar IRT $a$ and $b$ parameters representing item discrimination and location respectively are

$$\lambda = a, \tag{2.4}$$

and

$$-\frac{\zeta}{\lambda} = b. \tag{2.5}$$

The same transformations apply with the multivariate logit parameters of the NRM for each individual category (Baker, 1992). Thus, in the NRM, $a$ can be interpreted as a discrimination parameter in the usual way, whereas $b$ is a ratio of the slope and intercept parameters.

Baker (1992) cautions that the values of these $a$ and $b$ parameters do not have the same simple interpretation in the NRM as they have in the case of the dichotomous or ordered polytomous IRT models. This is because, in the latter two cases, the parameters define the functions that describe the boundaries between ordered categories (CBRFs), whereas the concept of ordered category boundaries is absent in the NRM case. In the NRM, the $a$ and $b$ parameters define the discrimination and location of the category functions (ICRFs) themselves where those functions need not be monotonic. Here, the shape and location of these functions depends on the way the parameter values from all the categories of an item combine.

This situation is similar to the case of the ordered polytomous Rasch model, where the denominator of the general expression (see Equations 1.3 and 1.4) is the sum of all the elements in the numerator and the ICRF for each category depends on the parameter values for all of an item's categories. However, in the ordered polytomous Rasch model, the numerator employs successive category boundary parameters to model a given category's response probability. The NRM, in contrast, has a separate multivariate logit for each item category.

The $b$ parameter in the NRM has also been discussed by De Ayala (1993), who defined it as the location on the $\theta$ continuum at which the ICRFs for adjacent categories cross. He shows that, in this definition,

$$b = \frac{\zeta_{(h-1)} - \zeta_n}{\lambda_h - \lambda_{(h-1)}}. \tag{2.6}$$

This interpretation is the same as that used in polytomous Rasch models, where it refers to the location of the CBRF between two adjacent categories. This interpretation of the parameter and the equation for obtaining it are clearly different from the $b$ parameter to which Baker refers, as expressed in Equation 2.5. The two authors are describing what amounts to different $b$ parameters. Indeed, Bock (1997b) refers to the location that De Ayala describes as a $b$ parameter simply as the crossing point of successive category response functions.

De Ayala's (1993) definition of the $b$ parameter and Bock's (1997b) use of the idea of successive categories implies some sort of category ordering for the NRM. In fact, Samejima (1988) states that the *purpose* of the NRM is to find the implicit ordering within initially unordered categorical data, and describes this as a strength of the model (Samejima, 1996). Although the former is not necessary (because implicit ordering is not required for the model to operate), it is true that the model can be used for this purpose. This will become clearer if we highlight some relevant relationships between the model parameters and the resulting ICRFs.

Typically, the category of an item that has the smallest value of $a$ among all the item's categories has a monotonically decreasing ICRF ranging from 1 at $\theta = -\infty$ to 0 at $\theta = \infty$. Conversely, an item's category with the largest value of $a$ has a monotonically increasing function from 0 at $\theta = -\infty$ to 1 at $\theta = \infty$. The remaining $m - 2$ functions usually will then be unimodal with tails asymptotically equal to zero (Baker, 1992; Bock, 1972, 1997b). An example of the ICRFs for a five-category item with $a = (0, -1, 1, 2, 3)$ and $c = (0, -1.5, 1.5, 1.5, 1.5)$ is given in Figure 2.1. The only time the general structure just outlined does not occur is when two categories have functions with the same slope parameter values and the same sign. In this case, the ICRFs of each category do not asymptote at 0 or 1 but at some other value in between (Baker, 1992). Thissen and Steinberg (1988) give an example of this occurring in a data set and plausibly interpret this occurrence to mean that the response categories do not differ in their relationship to $\theta$. The categories then differ only in overall level of relationship as represented by their respective intercept values.

However, in those cases where the values of the slope parameter are different across categories, Samejima (1972) showed that if these values are ordered, then the response probabilities for the categories will also be ordered. It is in this sense that Bock's (1997b) idea of successive categories and De Ayala's (1993) definition of the $b$ parameter have meaning.

More important, these characteristics of the $a$ parameter in the NRM mean that this model can be used to empirically test the ordering of categories for an item that is meant to have ordered categories. Such a test has

20

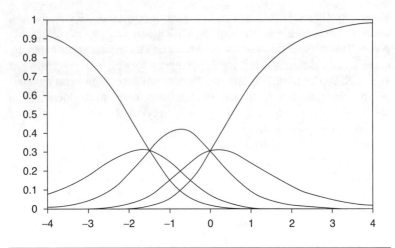

**Figure 2.1**　　NRM ICRFs for a Five-Category Item

two aspects. In the first place, it is to determine whether there actually is an ordering among the categories, whereas the second issue is whether the categories fall in the order expected. This application of the NRM is in addition to its use for explicitly modeling unordered polytomous data.

### Information

Baker (1992) and Mellenbergh (1995) note that the NRM employs the same general approach to information functions as do the ordered polytomous models, which in turn are based on the dichotomous case. In the case of the NRM, item information across the θ continuum can be formulated as

$$I_i(\theta) = \sum_{g=1}^{m} I_g(\theta) P_g(\theta) \tag{2.7}$$

where $I_g(\theta)$ is the amount of information provided by a specific response category and $P_g(\theta)$ is the probability of a respondent with trait level θ choosing the gth response category.

This shows that item information is comprised of the information provided by each category across the trait continuum. As with the dichotomous IRT models, this item information can be summed across all the items in a test to provide a test information function. In more general terms, this represents the information matrix. The uniform approach to information across dichotomous, ordered polytomous, and nominal response IRT models is extremely helpful in allowing comparisons of the level of measurement precision afforded by the different types of models.

## Relationship to Other IRT Models

The form of the general equation for the NRM is probably familiar due to its similarity to the general equation for the Rasch class of ordered polytomous models (Equation 1.3), although in the NRM, the numerator is a single expression and not a sum, as in the Rasch case. Nevertheless, it transpires that the NRM is, in fact, the most general divide-by-total model (Thissen & Steinberg, 1986). By imposing different linear restrictions on the $a_{i_g}s$ and $c_{i_g}s$, it is possible to express each of the polytomous Rasch models in terms of the nominal model.

This results in the interesting conclusion that there are really only two distinct types of polytomous IRT models (Thissen, 1991). One type is the divide-by-total family of models. These include Bock's (1972) nominal model and its variations (two of which will be described shortly), as well as the entire set of ordered polytomous Rasch models.

The other distinct type of polytomous IRT model is the family of difference models. The main example of such models is Samejima's graded response model, which is an extension of Thurstone's scaling approach. There are also a small number of variations of Samejima's basic model that will be introduced when that model is dealt with in more detail.

Interestingly, by employing a unique approach to developing the NRM, Mellenbergh (1995) shows that all of the common polytomous models for ordered data can be obtained as special cases of the NRM. In this work, he also highlights specific relationships among all the various polytomous models, which again draws attention to the different interpretations that are possible for polytomous item parameters.

## Variations

Because one of the primary uses for the NRM is with multiple-choice items, there is some concern that respondents might simply select a response at random. Two efforts were made to modify Bock's nominal model to account for the possibility of such behavior.

Samejima (1979b) initially extended Bock's (1972) model by incorporating a component for random responding (Baker, 1992). In her model, she did not estimate the value of the additional parameter, which accounts for responses that are not trait driven. Rather, she assumed that such responses were distributed with equal probability across all of an item's alternatives (Bock, 1997b) and therefore simply set the parameter value at $(1/m \times P_{i_o})$ distributed across all categories (Baker, 1992). Here, $m$ is, as usual, the number of response alternatives for an item, and $P_{i_0}$ is the strictly decreasing function for the "least plausible" category.

Thissen and Steinberg (1984), however, found that the empirical evidence contradicted Samejima's assumption that low-ability respondents randomly assigned their responses across the $m$ categories (Baker, 1992). They developed a model—also based on Bock's (1972) nominal model—in which the value of the random response parameter differs for each category of an item as a function of the other estimated parameters (Baker, 1992). This might occur, for example, in response to the position or labeling of the response alternatives (Bock, 1997b). Sympson (1983) presents a similar model that was not developed directly as a modification of Bock's model.

Thissen and Steinberg (1997) follow Baker's (1992) caution about the interpretation of $a$ and $b$ parameters in the NRM by suggesting that the parameters of their extension of the model are not, in fact, readily interpretable. They also note that estimation of the parameters can be extremely complicated. This leads Baker (1992) to suggest that, even though this may be an attractive model, the problems associated with its use imply that it is a case of overparameterization. Thissen and Steinberg (1984) suggest that even Bock's (1972) original model is sometimes too flexible, requiring that parameters be constrained in some way to actually make the model work (Thissen & Steinberg, 1984, 1988).

## A Practical Example

In our first practical example, we turn to a large-scale assessment program in which examinees were administered test questions in mathematics. This assessment program was administered to all 10th graders in a state located in the northeastern United States, and it was specifically designed to measure student mathematical achievement relative to a set of standards developed by state education officials. This assessment had eight test forms administered to more than 15,000 students and was part of an overall assessment program that also measured other content areas such as English, language arts, science, and social studies.

The assessment contains test questions of various formats, such as multiple-choice items, 4-point constructed response items, and writing prompts. To demonstrate how the nominal response model can be used to understand the relationship between an item and a student's latent trait, we isolated the multiple choice items from a single test form for the math assessment and used the computer program MULTILOG (Thissen, 1991) to estimate item parameters on the raw dataset. This involved a dataset with approximately 2,000 student response records.

TABLE 2.1
Parameter Values for a Math Item Using the Nominal Response Model

| | *i* | | | | |
|---|---|---|---|---|---|
| | *1* | *2* | *3* | *4* | Σ |
| $\lambda$ | −0.30 | 0.81 | − 0.31 | − 0.20 | 0.000 |
| $\zeta$ | 0.21 | 0.82 | − 0.09 | − 0.94 | 0.000 |
| $z\vert\theta = 1.50$ | −0.24 | 2.035 | − 0.555 | −1.24 | 0.000 |
| $z\vert\theta = -0.50$ | 0.36 | 0.415 | 0.065 | − 0.84 | 0.000 |
| $p\vert\theta = 1.50$ | 0.084 | 0.823 | 0.062 | 0.031 | 1.000 |
| $p\vert\theta = -0.50$ | 0.322 | 0.341 | 0.240 | 0.097 | 1.000 |

In Table 2.1 are found the item parameters for a particular item, along with the $z$ terms (see Equation 2.2) found using two arbitrary θ values (1.50 and −0.50). Notice how, in the last column, the sum of the $z$ terms is 0.00. This will occur for all values of θ. Also presented are the probabilities associated with each response option for $\theta = 1.50$ and $\theta = -0.50$. For examinees located at 1.5 along the θ continuum, they have a much higher probability of responding to the second alternative ($p$ = .823), which is the keyed response. However, for examinees located at −0.50, we see that they have very similar probabilities associated with the first and second categories, 0.322 and 0.341, respectively.

Using Equation 2.1 across the entire ability continuum ($-4.0 < \theta < 4.0$), we can obtain the category functions for this item. They are shown in Figure 2.2.

Even a cursory review of Figure 2.2 reveals how the NRM might be used in understanding how examinees along the trait continuum are interacting with this item. For example, the probability of choosing Option "B" (i.e., the keyed response) to this question increases as the examinee ability increases. Moreover, we see that less able examinees have an increasing tendency to choose Option "A," with a slightly lower probability of choosing Option "C." Option "D" is the only option that is generally flat across the ability continuum and has a value of around 0.10 for the least able examinees.

This practical example also shows how the NRM can be used to better understand items with unordered response options. Recall from the above description of the model that the height of the response functions is determined by the $\zeta(c)$ parameter and essentially represents the popularity of the response category, whereas the ordering of the categories can be inferred from the ordering of the $\lambda(a)$ parameter. Our example item shows that, in practice (Figure 2.2), results are rarely as clearly delineated as in theory

24

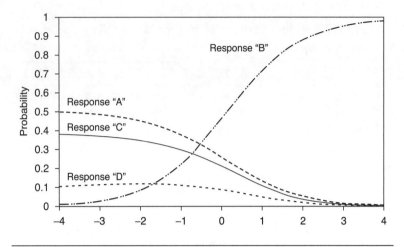

**Figure 2.2** ICRFs for a Multiple-Choice Ability Item Modeled by the NRM

(Figure 2.1). Nevertheless, looking at the parameter values in Table 2.1, in conjunction with the response functions in Figure 2.2 for each response option, is very informative. For example, they show that the keyed response (B) is also the most popular response, followed in order by Responses A, C, and D. In terms of implied category order, the example item parameters suggest that the highest-ability respondents will select the keyed response (B), with Response D the next most difficult category, followed by Responses A and C, which have very similar $\lambda$ parameters. The similarity of the slope parameters for Responses A and C results in a situation like that described above for the Thissen and Steinberg (1988) example, where neither of these categories asymptote at $p = 1$, even for very low-ability respondents. In fact, the ICRF for Response A asymptotes close to $p = .52$, whereas the function for Response C asymptotes close to $p = .47$. Therefore, the ICRF for Response D is the only unimodal function for this item, peaking at $q = -2.12$ on the trait continuum.

## 3. POLYTOMOUS RASCH MODELS

As described earlier, the way of dichotomizing and combining response data used in the Rasch class of polytomous models results in a general expression for the probability of a person responding in a given item category. This expression takes the form of Equation 1.3, which, in practice, expands in the manner shown in Equation 1.4. Masters and Wright (1984) demonstrate, more specifically, that virtually all Rasch polytomous models can take the form

$$P_{i_g}(\theta_n) = \frac{e^{\sum_{g=0}^{l}(\theta - b_{i_g})}}{\sum_{h=0}^{m} e^{\sum_{g=0}^{h}(\theta - b_{i_g})}}, \qquad (3.1)$$

where $\theta_n$ is the person trait level, $b_{i_g}$ and is the location parameter of the category boundary function for category $g$ of item $i$,

$1 = 0, \ldots, g$ (see Equation 1.4), and
$h = 0, \ldots, g, \ldots, m$.

Algebraically, the distinction between the different polytomous Rasch models can be described in terms of different expressions that can be used to represent the location parameter ($b$) of the category boundaries (Masters & Wright, 1984). Table 3.1 lists some of the possibilities. It should provide a useful reference as each model is described in turn.

TABLE 3.1
Variations on the General Form of the Rasch Model

Probability of responding in category $g$ of item $i$, conditional on $\theta$, is

$$P_{i_g} = \frac{e^{z_{i_g}}}{\sum e^{z_{i_h}}} = \frac{e^{\sum_{g=0}^{l}(\theta - b_{i_g})}}{\sum_{h=0}^{m} e^{\sum_{g=0}^{h}(\theta - b_{i_g})}},$$

where $h = 0, 1, \ldots, g, \ldots, m$ and $g$ represents a specific category being modeled; there are $m + 1$ response categories in the item;
$\theta$ represents the continuous latent trait (person location); and
$b$ is the category boundary location parameter.

When    $b_{i_g} = b_i$ this designates a dichotomous Rasch model.
$b_{i_g} = b_{i_g}$ this designates a partial credit model.
$b_{i_g} = b_i + \tau_g$ this designates a rating scale model.

## Partial Credit Model

Development of the partial credit model (PCM) is associated with the work of Masters (1982, 1988a, 1988c). Although it historically follows the development of the rating scale model, the PCM is a more general model and therefore will be introduced first. It is interesting to note that Rasch (1961) himself developed a polytomous model based on the measurement principles underlying his dichotomous model. The PCM, however, was not developed as an elaboration of Rasch's polytomous model (Masters, 1982).

The PCM is constructed in the manner described above for all ordered polytomous Rasch models. That is, it is built on the successive dichotomization of adjacent categories. In the PCM case, this results in a separate location parameter ($b$) for each category boundary ($g$) of each item ($i$), hence the notation for the PCM location parameter in Table 3.1. This approach allows the number of categories to vary from item to item in a test (Masters, 1982).

Masters (1982, 1988c; Wright & Masters, 1982) describes category boundaries between adjacent categories as steps that respondents must complete. These steps are ordered within an item as a consequence of the way in which the item is constructed. The archetypal example is a mathematics item where each part of the problem must be completed in sequence and where each successfully completed part of the problem (step) earns the respondent some credit.

The model is not, however, restricted to use with items that have response categories defined by component analytical problems. In fact, the PCM is suitable for use with any test format that provides a finite set of ordered response options (Masters & Wright, 1997). It should be noted, however, that the further one moves from the archetypal, multipart mathematics problem, the more effort is required to conceptualize the category boundaries as successive steps that must be completed in turn in order for respondents to locate themselves in a particular response category.

To illustrate this, consider an example that Masters (1982) provides, of a multiple-choice geography item. The response options have been explicitly ordered in terms of geographical proximity to the correct answer. The question is: "What is the capital of Australia?" The response options are

a. Wellington ... (1 pt)
b. Canberra ... (3 pts)
c. Montreal ... (0 pts)
d. Sydney ... (2 pts)

It is difficult to imagine that a respondent who selected the correct answer successively chose Wellington over Montreal, then Sydney over Wellington, and then Canberra over Sydney. Furthermore, it is difficult to accept that respondents with the lowest level of geographical ability would simply select the most wrong answer, Montreal, and fail to progress further. Such a response process is, however, implied by the step conceptualization of the model.

## Category Steps

Masters (1982) argues that an advantage of the Rasch dichotomization approach is that each CBRF (step) is independent of all others in an item. It transpires, however, that even with such items as the archetypal mathematics item, the PCM does not, in fact, validly model a response process characterized by sequential, independent steps between categories within an item. This fact also renders invalid the associated implication that the CBRF location parameters ($b_{i_g}$) indicate the difficulty, or trait level, of the respective boundaries (Molenaar, 1983; Verhelst & Verstralen, 1997).

Tutz (1990) provides a way to think about why the PCM cannot legitimately model a sequential steps process. In his explanation, he focuses on the fact that the PCM defines a step entirely locally, fixed at a point on the response scale that is delineated by the categories $g$ and $g - 1$. The first step (category boundary) in the PCM is therefore determined by a dichotomous Rasch model that assumes that the person's score is 1 or 2, but no other value. Thus, the next step from Category 2 to Category 3 cannot be thought of as taking place after the first step takes place because the first step allows only for the possibility that the outcome is 1 or 2. It does not accommodate the possibility of subsequent responses. This means that to model sequential steps, the PCM would, in a sense, need to be able to see into the future and know the outcome of subsequent steps (Tutz, 1990). This explanation neatly encapsulates Verhelst and Verstralen's (1997) demonstration that the PCM models a series of dependent binary variables.

Ultimately, Masters (1988c) agrees that the steps notion had been misinterpreted in early PCM research and development, warning that the location parameter of the category boundaries (steps) *cannot* be interpreted as the "difficulties" or location of independent parts of an item. Instead, he highlights the important fact that even though the boundary dichotomizations (steps) are locally defined, they occur in the context of an entire item and therefore are not completely independent.

Nevertheless, the notion of item steps has proved to be stubbornly enduring in the PCM literature, perhaps because of its intuitive appeal. It probably also persists because it was such a central part of the early expositions of the model (e.g., Masters, 1982, 1988c; Masters & Wright, 1984; Wright & Masters, 1982).

The principal advantage of constructing an ordered polytomous IRT model on the basis of the local comparisons that define the adjacent category dichotomizations ($b_{i_g}$) is that this approach allows parameter separability (Molenaar, 1983). That is, the person and item parameters can be conditioned out of the estimation of the respective alternate parameter. This occurs because this type of dichotomization, with the associated method for subsequently combining the category boundary information, provides easily obtainable sufficient statistics for each type of parameter (Masters, 1982). The result is that specific objectivity is maintained in this model (Masters, 1982, 1988c; Molenaar, 1983), which, in turn, is why this type of model qualifies as a Rasch model. Glas and Verhelst (1989) suggest that the advantages of having a model with parameter separability, in most cases, outweigh the difficulties arising from the complicated parameter interpretation.

**The Mathematical Model**

The PCM is described mathematically by the general form for all polytomous Rasch models shown in Equation 1.3. By incorporating a location parameter (*b*) for each category boundary (*g*) and each item (*i*), we obtain a flexible model where categories can vary in number and structure across items within a test (Masters, 1982). That is, even for items with the same number of categories, the boundary locations are free to vary from item to item. As described in the prelude to Table 3.1, the Rasch approach to combining category boundary information results in a general equation for the probability of responding in a specific item category ($P_{i_g}$) for the PCM, contingent on θ, of the form

$$P_{i_g} = \frac{e^{\sum_{g=0}^{l}(\theta - b_{i_g})}}{\sum_{h=0}^{m} e^{\sum_{g=0}^{h}(\theta - b_{i_g})}}. \tag{3.1}$$

Each adjacent pair of response categories is modeled by a simple logistic ogive with the same slope (Masters & Wright, 1984; Wright & Masters, 1982) to produce category boundaries that differ only in location. In other words, the CBRFs are obtained by applying the dichotomous Rasch model to each successive, adjacent pair of response categories for an item. The dichotomous model used to obtain CBRFs takes the form

$$P_{i_{g|g-1,g}} = \frac{e^{(\theta - b_{i_g})}}{1 + e^{(\theta - b_{i_g})}}, \tag{3.2}$$

where, in this case, because CBRFs are being modeled, the response probability is designated $P_{i_{g|g-1_g}}$, representing the probability of responding in category *g* rather than *g* − 1, given that the response must be in *g* or *g* − 1, with *g* = 1, 2, . . . , *m*. Equation 3.2 is identical to the usual equation for the dichotomous Rasch model except for the subscript on *b*, which differentiates the item category boundaries. Equation 3.2 plus the requirement that a respondent must respond in one of the $m + 1$ categories leads to the general expression for PCM ICRFs shown in Equation 3.1. Furthermore, for notational convenience,

$$\sum_{g=0}^{0} (\theta - b_{i_g}) \equiv 0, \qquad (3.3)$$

so that

$$\sum_{g=0}^{h} (\theta - b_{i_g}) \equiv \sum_{g=1}^{h} (\theta - b_{i_g}). \qquad (3.4)$$

A complete derivation of Equation 3.1 is given in Masters and Wright (1984). In Equation 3.1, 1 is the count of the boundary locations up to the category under consideration. The numerator contains only the locations of the boundaries prior to the specific category, $g$, being modeled. The denominator is the sum of all $m + 1$ possible numerators (Wright & Masters, 1982). An example of what this would look like if one were modeling the third category of a five-category item is shown in Equation 1.4.

The use of simple counts as the basic data for the model is a distinguishing characteristic of Rasch models (Wright & Masters, 1982). This is contrasted with other models that weight category scores, typically by employing a discrimination parameter when modeling category boundaries. The Rasch approach of using simple counts makes it possible to obtain the probability of a given response vector, conditional on $\theta$, without reference to the $\theta$ level of the person responsible for the responses (Wright & Masters, 1982). This demonstrates the separability of the person and item parameters, and this approach can be extended to an entire response matrix to show that all item and person parameters can be estimated independently of each other (Wright & Masters, 1982). This is part of the notion of specific objectivity.

An interesting consequence of this type of parameterization is that, for any given item calibration dataset, there must be responses in every available response category of an item. Otherwise, it is not possible to estimate values for all item parameters (Masters & Wright, 1997). This is a feature of all polytomous Rasch models. It suggests that polytomous Rasch models may suffer in practical testing situations from a problem similar to that described by Drasgow, Levine, Tsien, William, and Mead (1995) for the NRM, namely, that it is difficult to implement in sparse data settings. The unusual situation also follows that the different boundary location parameter estimates for an item are typically based on different numbers of respondents. This has interesting implications for differing precision in the estimates of the model's item parameters. Standard errors will always be worse for parameters that model categories with fewer respondents in a manner directly comparable to the situation Tutz (1997) describes for his sequential model.

## Information

The notion of statistical item or test information is rarely employed in the Rasch measurement literature where the issue of measurement precision is subordinated to issues surrounding measurement validity. This distinction is blurred by Lord's (1980) description of information as a form of validity. However, common usage in the IRT literature concentrates on information as an indicator of measurement precision, whereas model fit and issues concerning the plausibility of a model for a specific dataset are key elements of the measurement validity discussions more common in the Rasch literature. The deemphasis of information in the Rasch literature is at least partly due to the fact that, in the dichotomous case, the fixed slope parameter of the Rasch model results in all items having identical information functions. Of course, test information still varies across tests with different items. In any case, Smith (1987) notes that Rasch measurement tends to employ an index called reliability of person separation ($R_p$) instead of CTT reliability and in preference to test information for assessing measurement precision.

Nevertheless, it is entirely possible to calculate item information for the PCM in exactly the same manner as for other IRT models, that is, as the inverse of the variance of the maximum likelihood estimate of $\theta$, evaluated across $\theta$ (Mellenbergh, 1995). Wright and Masters (1982, Chapter 8) provide plots of measurement error at the test level in terms of variance, which, as Mellenbergh's (1995) comment indicates, is the inverse of test information.

The earliest use of the concept of statistical information in a PCM context was the work of Dodd (1984). She derived the formulae for test and item information for the PCM based on Birnbaum's (1968) definitions of item and test information functions, and on Samejima's (1969) application of Birnbaum's formulation to the GRM. This amounted to a close approximation of Samejima's ICRF-based equations to the PCM ICRFs.

Details of Samejima's (1969) approach to calculating information will be discussed in more detail in the upcoming chapter on her models. There is also another approach to calculating information based on PCM IRFs rather than ICRFs. Explaining the practical steps involved in calculating item information in this alternative approach requires reparameterization of the PCM in a form that differs from Masters' (1982) parameterization of the model. This particular parameterization forms the basis of Andrich's (1978b) development of the RSM. Therefore, a detailed description of this approach to calculating item information in the polytomous Rasch model context will be provided as part of the later description of the RSM. Dodd and Koch (1994) found that, empirically, both approaches produce almost identical results.

## Relationship to Other IRT Models

As one of the most general unidimensional, polytomous Rasch models, the PCM can be considered—conceptually and structurally—as the basis for almost all other unidimensional polytomous Rasch models. This includes the Rating Scale, Binomial Trials, and Poisson Counts models (Wright & Masters, 1982), as well as other models for rating data developed by Andrich (1982) and by Rost (1988a). Furthermore, in the special case of an item with two ordered categories, the PCM becomes the dichotomous Rasch model. These are all divide-by-total models in Thissen and Steinberg's (1986) taxonomy. Among early polytomous Rasch models the only examples that are not in the PCM family of models are the multidimensional polytomous model developed by Rasch (1961) himself and a unidimensional version of this model developed by Andersen (1973). A multidimensional model is simply one that simultaneously models more than one latent trait for each respondent. Recent work however has involved extending polytomous Rasch models in various ways including approaches that generalize Rasch's (1961) early model itself into a much more comprehensive framework. These Rasch model extensions will be introduced in upcoming sections following the introduction of the RSM.

Samejima (1972, 1988, 1996) argues that the PCM itself represents a special case of the NRM. She demonstrates how this is the case in the context of her general framework for items with multiple responses. It is worth noting that Samejima's argument regarding the PCM and the NRM reaches the same conclusion as Mellenbergh (1995), even if the form of their arguments differ.

It is important to be aware that the PCM is not a simplified version of Samejima's (1969) usual graded response model (GRM). This is in marked contrast to the dichotomous case where the Rasch model can be considered a simplified variation on the 2PL and 3PL IRT models.

## Variations

Because the PCM is among the most general of the class of Rasch models described in this text, it could be argued that all other unidimensional polytomous Rasch models are variations of the PCM. Although this may be technically true, the rating scale model (RSM) elaborated by Andrich

(1978b) predates the development of the PCM. It also contains features that warrant a separate discussion.

The binomial trials and Poisson counts models, however, are true variants of the PCM. The binomial trials model is designed to accommodate data from a response format that allows respondents a fixed number ($m$) of attempts at an item (Masters & Wright, 1984; Wright & Masters, 1982). The number of successes a respondent has on a given item represents the "category" that he or she scores for the item, such as hitting a target 7 times in 10 attempts. The Poisson counts model extends the idea of the binomial trials model to the situation where there is no finite limit to the number of successes (or failures) a person might have at a given task (Masters & Wright, 1984; Wright & Masters, 1982). Rasch (1960) developed this model himself to analyze reading errors, where there was no fixed number of errors that a student could make. These two models modify the PCM by adjusting the way the location parameter is represented in ways analogous to the examples listed in Table 3.1.

Another way to modify the PCM is to insert into the model a positive discrimination parameter ($a$) that is free to vary from the implied $a = 1$ of the usual PCM. This would allow the discrimination for the boundary location functions (CBRFs) to vary from boundary to boundary. In effect, this means modeling the CBRFs with the 2PL dichotomous model instead of the dichotomous Rasch model. Note again that this does not result in a Thurstone/ Samejima type of polytomous model because it is still only adjacent categories that are being dichotomized.

Discrimination parameter values can vary three ways across a set of polytomous items. Most generally, the parameters could vary across boundary locations within an item as well as across equivalent locations in different items—where items have the same number of categories. Alternatively, the discrimination parameter could be fixed to be the same for each equivalent boundary location ($g$) for all items in a test (Hemker, 1996, Chapter 5). This would again require that all items in a test had the same number of categories. The third alternative is for discriminations to be held constant across CBRFs within an item but for them to be free to vary across items. Items would again be free to vary in the number of categories per item. This variation of the PCM describes the rationale behind Muraki's (1992) generalized partial credit model (GPCM). This particular variation has also been called Thissen and Steinberg's ordinal model (TSOM) by Maydeu-Olivares, Drasgow, and Mead (1994).

The features of the GPCM that pertain to its scoring function formulation will be explored further in the context of the upcoming representation of the RSM. In contrast to the GPCM, the TSOM (Maydeu-Olivares et al., 1994; Thissen & Steinberg, 1986) is formulated explicitly in the form of

Equation 3.1. It simply substitutes a 2PL model for the dichotomous Rasch model when modeling CBRFs, with the additional constraint that the discrimination parameters be equal across CBRFs within an item. Wilson (1992; Wilson & Adams, 1993) developed the ordered partition model (OPM) as an extension of the PCM. The OPM is designed to model data that are neither entirely nominal nor completely ordered. In particular, it is envisioned as appropriate for items that have ordered levels, but where there may be a number of nominal response categories within any given level. Wilson suggests that the OPM may be particularly relevant for data resulting from the performance assessment paradigm in education.

Wilson and Masters (1993) developed a procedure for modeling data with the PCM when one or more available item categories are not used. This could occur either when a category is observed to be without responses in an empirical setting, or when a category is predefined to be empty on theoretical grounds in a particular application of an item. Categories that are left unused are called null categories. Such a model may be of considerable importance because, as Ludlow and Haley (1992) note, PCM estimation typically obtains item parameter estimates from one nonzero frequency (non-null) category to the next. Masters and Wright (1984) address this issue by pointing out that all the item parameters for the model can be estimated only if there are data in each of the available response categories. This, in turn, means that the boundary parameters that are estimated may not be those presented to test respondents because null categories are essentially automatically collapsed into subsequent categories in this process.

Wilson and Masters' (1993) modeling of null categories is accomplished by reparameterizing the PCM of Masters (1982) in a manner similar to the way the NRM is parameterized. Specifically, rather than being constructed on the basis of category boundaries, item parameters are provided to model ICRFs directly, using weight and location parameters. The weight parameters are considered to be the slope parameters in the NRM and other similar formulations. The null categories are then modeled by setting the weight and location parameters for those categories to both equal zero. By incorporating null categories into the response model, one is able to avoid the need to collapse categories, which may be inappropriate for polytomous Rasch models (Jansen & Roskam, 1986; Rasch, 1966; Roskam, 1995; Roskam & Jansen, 1989).

The approach outlined by Wilson and Masters (1993) for handling null categories in the PCM can be extended to the entire family of polytomous Rasch models. A particularly valuable potential use for this approach is in handling sparse data conditions to which polytomous Rasch models may be particularly susceptible.

## PCM Summary

Masters and Wright (1997) suggest that the strength of the PCM is its simplicity, which derives from applying a dichotomous Rasch model to each pair of adjacent item categories. The result is a polytomous IRT model with only two parameters, where both are location parameters; one for items, $b_{i_g}$, and one for people, $\theta_j$. As we have seen, the dichotomizing approach employed in this model makes it sensitive to sparse data conditions, which may be common in practice. Furthermore, the resulting item location parameters have ambiguous meaning. A practical consequence of employing this particular type of boundary location parameters can also be seen in the example that Masters and Wright (1997) provide. In their example, they show how regions of a trait continuum are defined by different essay graders. However, to do this, they must use Thurstone/Samejima CBRF location parameters because the PCM $b_{i_g}$ cannot be used for this purpose.

Masters and Wright (1997) also highlight the fact that the algebraic formulation of the PCM gives it the statistical properties of a Rasch model. This means that it has separable person and item parameters. Therefore, it is specifically objective within and between person and item parameter comparisons and has the sufficient statistics for all model parameters required for conjoint additivity and fundamental measurement. It could be argued that the possibility of fundamental measurement might outweigh the weaknesses of the PCM, if the model can be shown to fit a given dataset.

## Rating Scale Model

Items used in psychological testing contexts such as attitude, interest, personality surveys, inventories, or questionnaires often have a consistent structural form across all of the items for a given measurement instrument. Often, this is a Likert or similar type of rating scale format where people are asked to respond to an item using a predefined set of responses and where the same set of response alternatives is applied to all the items in the test. A typical example of such a response format is when people are asked to respond to each item on a test using a 5-point scale ranging from *strongly disagree,* through *neutral,* to *strongly agree.*

The rating scale model (RSM) is uniquely suited to this type of response format. The fundamental assumption of the model, which distinguishes it from other polytomous IRT models, is that the use of a single rating response format across items in a test implies that the response format is intended to function in the same way (i.e., be consistently applied) across all items, because the categories have a constant definition. The implied intent is reflected in the model by the exposition of a common parametric form for all the items using a given rating scale. The result is that, in the RSM, any given category on the response scale is modeled to be the same "size" across all items, although within an item on the scale, the different response categories need not be the same size as each other.

Thus, in contrast to the PCM, all items being modeled by the RSM in a given setting must have the same number of categories, and the categories must, in effect, have the same set of labels across the items. Of course, if items in a test use two rating scales with different numbers of categories, or if the categories have different labels, they are, by definition, different rating scales, and the basic assumption of the RSM would apply to each scale separately.

Masters (1988c; Masters & Wright, 1984) sometimes describes the RSM in terms of a constrained version of the PCM. Although this is formally correct, the RSM also contains several distinctive features. First, the RSM, as an explicated mathematical model, predates the PCM by several years. Furthermore, although the PCM was not developed as an elaboration of Rasch's (1961) polytomous model, the RSM is explicitly linked to Rasch's model. Indeed, the model's originators describe the RSM as a special case of Rasch's (1961) multidimensional, polytomous model (Andersen, 1997; Andrich, 1978a).

Another feature of the RSM is that it is presented in a mathematical form that facilitates a fuller understanding of some especially interesting elements of polytomous items and IRT models, specifically with respect to the notion of discrimination. Finally, the RSM is described without reference to the notion of item steps. Instead, category boundaries are described as *thresholds,* which is the more common term in attitudinal scaling. This change of terminology also helps reduce the temptation to think of the boundaries as embodying independent, sequential dichotomizations, which is so closely attached to the steps concept.

The thresholds still represent locally defined dichotomizations in keeping with the polytomous Rasch approach to defining category boundaries. However, rather than describing these boundaries as independent, sequential steps, Andrich (1978b) conceives the response process in terms of respondents making simultaneous, independent, dichotomous choices at each threshold. This leads to some interesting possibilities. For example, when there are four possible responses to a three-category item, a person could respond positively at both thresholds (choose Category 3), respond negatively at both thresholds (choose Category 1), respond positively at the first and negatively at the second threshold (choose Category 2), or respond negatively at the first and positively at the second threshold. This last response set is logically inconsistent, and Andrich (1978b) suggests that respondents recognize this and respond accordingly. Naturally, the possibilities for logically inconsistent responses grow dramatically as items with more categories are considered.

## The Mathematical Model

The RSM is a special case of Rasch's (1961) polytomous model in that it begins with the postulate that a single dimension is modeled in contrast to Rasch's general model, which is multidimensional in terms of both the person parameter and with respect to item response categories (Andrich, 1978a; Rasch, 1961). Andersen (1973) built the foundations for the RSM by providing an estimation method for the item parameters of Rasch's (1961) model when it is applied to questionnaire items. This included a discussion of how to obtain the sufficient statistics needed for the estimation procedure.

Andrich (1978b) suggests that his own work complements that of Andersen by providing a substantive interpretation of various parameters in Rasch's (1961) model to go with the statistical properties that Andersen provides. This is important because Rasch (1961) describes his parameters in only the most general theoretical terms. Specifically, Andrich (1978b) describes how the category coefficients of Rasch's model can be interpreted in terms of thresholds on a latent continuum, where thresholds are a form of category boundaries, whereas Rasch's scoring function is interpreted in terms of discriminations at the thresholds.

## Model Parameters

Because the PCM was not developed with reference to Rasch's (1961) model, we have not yet been introduced to the category coefficient and scoring function parameters. In this section, we will introduce these parameters through a rearrangement of model parameters that we have already seen. Recall that from Table 3.1, the general equation for the RSM is obtained as

$$P_{i_g} = \frac{e^{\sum_{g=0}^{l}[\theta-(b_i+\tau_g)]}}{\sum_{h=0}^{m} e^{\sum_{g=0}^{h}[\theta-(b_i+\tau_g)]}}, \tag{3.5}$$

where $h = 0, 1, \ldots, g, \ldots, m$, with $g$ representing the specific category being modeled from among $m + 1$ categories. This shows that in the RSM, the usual polytomous Rasch category boundary parameter $(b_{i_g})$ is decomposed into two elements, $b_i$ and $\tau_g$. The $b_i$ parameter becomes an item location parameter that is estimated for each individual item in a test, whereas the $\tau_g$ are the threshold parameters that define the boundary between the categories of the rating scale, relative to each item's trait location. That is, the $\tau_g$ tell you how far each category boundary is from the location parameter. These parameters are estimated once for an entire set of items employing a given rating scale, in keeping with the rating scale assumption described above. Given the response format in question and the fact that the $\tau_g$ are estimated once for an entire set of items, Andrich (1978a) requires that the threshold parameters be ordered, in contrast to PCM category boundaries.

The form of the RSM given in Equation 3.5 reflects Masters' (1988c) conceptualization of the RSM as a constrained version of the PCM. Andrich (1978b), however, shows that it is useful to expand the numerator in Equation 3.5 and that this becomes particularly meaningful if a discrimination parameter $(a)$ is explicitly included. Equation 3.5 then becomes

$$
P_{i_g} = \frac{e^{\sum_{g=0}^{l} [a_g(\theta - (b_i + \tau_g))]}}{\sum_{h=0}^{m} e^{\sum_{g=0}^{h} [a_g(\theta - (b_i + \tau_g))]}}. \tag{3.6}
$$

Note that the discrimination parameter is indexed only with respect to the relevant category boundary $(g)$. Andrich (1978b) points out that it is quite possible, within this mathematical framework, to also index the discrimination by individual items $(a_{i_g})$. However, because the Rasch model requires items to have the same discrimination, this idea is not pursued (Andrich, 1978b).

Expanding the numerator of Equation 3.6 produces

$$
\sum_{g=0}^{l} [a_g(\theta - (b_i - \tau_g))] = \sum_{g=0}^{l} -a_g \tau_g + \sum_{g=0}^{l} a_g(\theta - b_i). \tag{3.7}
$$

If we then define parameters $\phi_g$ and $\kappa_g$ as a set of sums of relevant values up to the specific category being modeled at any time, such that

$$
\phi_g = \sum_{g=0}^{l} a_g, \tag{3.8}
$$

and

$$
\kappa_g = -\sum_{g=0}^{l} a_g \tau_g, \tag{3.9}
$$

then the general form of the RSM (Equation 3.5) becomes

$$P_{i_g} = \frac{e^{[\kappa_g + \phi_g(\theta - b_i)]}}{\sum_{h=0}^{m} e^{[\kappa_h + \phi_h(\theta - b_i)]}}, \tag{3.10}$$

where $h = 0, 1, \ldots, g, \ldots, m$ for $m + 1$ categories and $\phi_g = \kappa_g = 0$ for $g = 0$. Also note that there is now no longer a summation sign in the numerator of Equation 3.10 and only one in the denominator, in contrast to Equation 3.5.

Equation 3.10 is the unidimensional form of Rasch's (1961) polytomous model where the $g$ are the category coefficient parameters and the $\kappa_g$ are the $\phi_g$ scoring function parameters (Andrich, 1978b; Masters, 1982). The interpretation provided by Andrich (1978b) for these parameters is that Rasch's category coefficients are a negative sum of the products of the threshold locations ($\tau_g$) and their respective discriminations ($a_g$) up to the category ($g$) under consideration. The scoring functions, in turn, are simply a sum of the threshold discriminations up to $g$. More generally, Andersen (1973) notes Rasch's description of the $\phi_g$ as the scoring values of the response categories, that is, the category scores. Andrich (1978b) here shows what comprises these category scores.

In this form, however, Equation 3.10 still describes a very general model because, as Rasch (1961, p. 330; Fischer & Ponocny, 1995) intended, the scoring functions must be estimated from the data. Note that this form of Equation 3.10 also implies that within a legitimate Rasch model, discrimination can vary from threshold to threshold; or, in the more general terminology used so far, it is possible for category boundary discriminations to vary within an item.

Equation 3.10 can be simplified by requiring that all threshold discriminations be the same, such that $a_1 = a_2 \cdots = a_m = a$ then

$$\phi_g = a \times g, \tag{3.11}$$

and

$$\kappa_g = -\sum_{g=0}^{l} a\tau_g, \tag{3.12}$$

and threshold discrimination becomes a constant so that the scoring function need no longer be estimated. Indeed, the magnitude of $a$ is no longer an issue because it is absorbed into the person, item, and threshold parameters (Andrich, 1978b). The key RSM requirement is simply that the category score values in $\phi$ increase by a constant, a condition that Equation 3.11

fulfills. Absorbing the value of $a$ into the remaining model parameters essentially fixes the threshold discrimination value equal to 1.0. The category coefficient then simply becomes the negative sum of the threshold location values up to the category in question, and the scoring function becomes the number of thresholds crossed or, in our more general terminology, the number of category boundaries traversed. When the $m + 1$ categories are numbered in the usual manner from 0, 1, . . . , $m$, then the scoring function values for any given category are simply the category score or category label value. Under this simplification,

$$\phi_g = g, \tag{3.13}$$

and

$$\kappa_g = -\sum_{g=0}^{l} \tau_g. \tag{3.14}$$

Equation 3.10 with the scoring functions ($\phi_g$) and category coefficients ($\kappa_g$) defined as in Equations 3.13 and 3.14, respectively, is the usual form of the RSM. Equation 3.13 is described by Andrich (1978b) as an integral scoring function, although it has become known in the literature as a linear integer scoring function.

This form of the scoring function is intuitively appealing because it corresponds to the usual Likert-type scoring approach of weighting successive category responses by the respective category scores, which are usually successive integers. It also has important statistical consequences. Andersen (1973, 1977) showed that the scoring function must take the form of Equation 3.11 for there to be a real valued sufficient statistic for $\theta$ that is independent of the item parameters. Because Equation 3.13 also has this form, it has the same property. Andersen (1977) calls this "equidistant scoring" (p. 69). Andrich (1978a, 1978b) stresses that the scoring function approach defined in Equation 3.14, where successive categories are scored with successive integers, is a result of having equal discriminations at the thresholds and not equal distances between thresholds.

## Sufficient Statistics and Other Considerations

The actual sufficient statistic for $\theta$ is simply a person's total score (Andrich, 1978a), or equivalently in this formulation, the number of thresholds, across all items, that the person has crossed (Andrich, 1978b). Furthermore, the total number of responses, across all people and all items, in the category $g$ is a sufficient statistic for $\kappa_g$. Also, the sum of all the responses to an item weighted by category score, that is, the total score for an item $i$, is a sufficient statistic for $b_i$, the item location parameter. Andersen (1983) presents a more general RSM model that does not require category scores to increase by a constant value. Andersen (1983, 1995) is careful to point out, however, that in more general Rasch models, with unequal threshold discriminations resulting in category scores that do not increase uniformly, one must have known category scores. To be more specific, it is not possible to estimate the category score values (scoring function) within the Rasch framework. This is because it is not possible to obtain the requisite distribution-free sufficient statistics for item parameter estimation unless the values of $a_g$ are known, or prespecified. Of course, the usual RSM linear integer scoring function involves prespecified discrimination values. They are essentially prespecified to equal 1.0. It is interesting to note that when the scoring function is not the linear integer function, ICRFs are no longer symmetrical. Furthermore, category boundaries are now also no longer the location on the trait continuum where there is an equal probability of responding in either of the adjacent categories (Muraki, 1993).

Another feature of the scoring function formulation of the RSM is that it sheds light on the notion of collapsing categories. Andersen (1977) shows that having the same category score for two categories collapses the categories. Andrich (1978b) points out that this situation, where $\phi_{g+1} = \phi_g$, results when $a_{g+1} = 0$, meaning that the threshold does not discriminate, and therefore, the categories on either side can be pooled. This is a consequence of the fact that the $\phi$ effectively function to order the answer categories (Andersen, 1973). If successive $\phi$ values are not ordered, the answer categories will not be ordered, but rather will be nominal categories in the sense of Bock's (1972) NRM.

The process of elaborating the scoring function formulation of the RSM, that is, going from Equation 3.5 to Equation 3.10, therefore helps clarify the role of category scores, thresholds, and item and threshold discrimination in polytomous Rasch models. It also shows that it is possible to reparameterize formally identical models in strikingly different ways.

In summary, the RSM is composed of a location parameter for each item $(b_i)$ and a set of parameters for the response alternatives across all items in a test or questionnaire $(\tau_g)$ that requires estimation. Thus, the RSM has fewer parameters to estimate than the PCM [$n$ item location parameters + $m$ threshold (category boundary) parameters versus $n \times m$ item (category boundary) parameters for the PCM]. Masters (1988c) warns that this parsimony may come at the cost of lost information about interactions between items and response alternatives that may be subtle but psychologically interesting. It also means that the only modeled difference between items

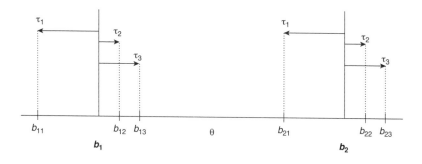

**Figure 3.1**    Graphical Representation of a Set of RSM Threshold Parameters
Applied to Two Hypothetical Items

with the RSM is their location, $b_i$, on the $\theta$ scale (Masters, 1988c). This is
shown graphically for two hypothetical, four-category items in Figure 3.1.
The ends of the arrows indicate the category boundary locations relative to
each item's location. Note that each boundary ($\tau_g$) is the same distance from
the location parameter of each item. The specific trait scale location for
each boundary is indicated on the ordinate by $b_{i_g}$, which also represents the
point on the $\theta$ scale at which the ICRFs for the relevant categories would
intersect if they were plotted.

Masters (1988a) suggests that, in addition to modeling rating scale items,
the RSM might also be useful when there are insufficient data to provide
reliable estimates for all of the parameters required to model the PCM.
Wilson (1988) notes that applying the RSM to items that have no data in
some of their categories (typically, extreme categories) essentially results in
the model imputing parameters for those categories from data from the other
items in the analysis. This, of course, is the case whether one is attempting
to resolve PCM parameter estimation problems as described by Masters
(1988a) or legitimately applying the RSM to sparse rating scale-type data.

## Information

Understanding the concept of information with respect to polytomous
Rasch models is facilitated by the scoring function formulation of these
models. Although this formulation has, thus far, been shown only with
respect to the RSM, its application to the PCM and the GPCM follow in
a straightforward manner, as will be shown later in the RSM variations
section. A useful starting point with respect to information is the realization
that the scoring function formulation of these models allows us to easily
calculate an IRF for a polytomous item.

## Expected Values and Response Functions

The ease of calculating a polytomous item IRF follows from the fact that an IRF can be thought of as describing the rate of change of the expected value of an item response as a function of the change in θ relative to an item's location $b_i$ (Andrich, 1988a). More succinctly, this can be thought of as a regression of the item score onto the trait scale (Chang & Mazzeo, 1994; Lord, 1980).

In the case of a dichotomous item, the expected value of a score for an item is the regression of the positive response on θ, which is the usual IRF for that item (e.g., Figure 1.1). From this perspective, a negative response equates with failure to score. In more formal terms, the expected value of response $x$ for item $i$ is

$$E[X_i] = (P_i = 1|\theta). \qquad (3.15)$$

As noted earlier, in dichotomous IRT models, the IRF provides the probability of responding in a given category, a function that is performed by the ICRFs in polytomous IRT models. However, if we maintain the regression, or the expected value, description of an IRF, then it is possible to obtain an IRF for polytomous items also. This is a single function, generally monotonically increasing in θ, that describes the "conditional mean of item scores at a given θ" (Muraki, 1997, p. 156). The scoring function for a polytomous item makes it a simple matter to obtain the function for this conditional mean/IRF/expected value. When the usual linear integer scoring function is employed, the expected value of response $x$ (where $x \in g = 0$, $1, \ldots, m$) for item $i$ is

$$E[X_i] = \sum_g g P_{i_g}(\theta), \qquad (3.16)$$

that is, it is a weighted sum of ICRF values (Chang & Mazzeo, 1994) where the ICRF values are weighted by the scoring function.

As we will see later, one may have reason to use a scoring function other than the usual linear integer function. In that case, a more general form of the expected value is

$$E[T_i] = \sum_{g=1}^{m} T_g P_{i_g}(\theta) = \overline{T_i}(\theta), \qquad (3.17)$$

where $T_g$ is the (not necessarily linear integer) scoring function for categories $g = 0, 1, \ldots, m$, and $\overline{T_g}(\theta)$ is the notation for item $i$'s conditional mean given θ, that is, its IRF.

**Response Functions and Information**

Andrich (1988a) notes that the discrimination of a polytomous item, at any value of θ, is the rate of change of the IRF given by $E[X_i]$ , with respect to θ. Item information in the IRT context is directly related to item discrimination, such that $I_i(\theta)$ = Squared IRF Slope/Conditional Variance, where $I_i(\theta)$ represents item information and IRF slope is synonymous with discrimination. Now that we have a ready method for obtaining an IRF for a polytomous item, the equation for item information follows directly.

Masters and Evans (1986) give this form of the equation for item information as where the squared component on the right side of the difference

$$\frac{\partial E[X_i]}{\partial \theta} = V[X_i] = \sum_{g=1}^{m} T_g^2 P_{i_g} - \left( \sum_{g=1}^{m} T_g P_{i_g} \right)^2 , \tag{3.18}$$

symbol can be recognized from Equation 3.17 as the IRF. Category information then can be obtained as a partition of the item information due to a given category (Muraki, 1993). That is,

$$I_{i_g}(\theta) = P_{i_g}(\theta) I_i(\theta). \tag{3.19}$$

Muraki (1993) provides an expanded version of Equation 3.18 incorporating the notion that item information is a sum of category information for the categories of an item. Thus, Equation 3.18 is multiplied by $P_{i_g}$, giving category information by Equation 3.19, and then summed across categories to give

$$I_i(\theta) = \sum_{g=0}^{m} P_{i_g}(\theta) \left[ \sum_{g=0}^{m} T_g^2 P_{i_g} - \left( \sum_{g=0}^{m} T_g P_{i_g} \right)^2 \right] , \tag{3.20}$$

$$= \sum_{g=0}^{m} [T_g - \overline{T_i}(\theta)]^2 P_{i_g} , \tag{3.21}$$

where Equation 3.21 is a simplification of Equation 3.20 (Muraki, 1993).

These two equations describe item information for a polytomous model that does not have a separate item discrimination parameter, such as the PCM. In the case of models such as the GPCM, which have an additional item discrimination parameter, item information is obtained by multiplying either equation by item discrimination squared, that is, $a_i^2$ (Muraki, 1993). Similarly, these equations all have information functions on the logistic metric. If equivalence with the normal ogive metric is desired, then these equations must also be multiplied by the square of the scaling factor, $D$ (where $D = 1.702$). So, for example, item information in the form of Equation 3.21 that is modified for items with an item discrimination parameter and also modified to place information on the normal ogive metric would take the form

$$= D^2 a_i^2 \sum_{g=0}^{m} [T_g - \overline{T_i}(\theta)]^2 P_{i_g}. \qquad (3.22)$$

Although the notion of statistical information is not a feature of usual Rasch model discussion, Andrich (1978a, 1979) does refer to the large sample standard errors of maximum likelihood parameter estimates for the RSM. In the case of the person parameter estimate, this is simply the negative inverse of the square root of the usual item information function. Andrich's discussion of the standard errors serves to highlight the possibility of obtaining information functions for any model parameter (not just $\theta$). This is an issue rarely discussed in any IRT literature, although conceptually, this approach would provide an indication of the "measurement" precision of item, as well as the usual person, parameters. Interestingly, more recent discussions of generalized Rasch models (e.g., Adams & Wilson, 1996) explicitly refer to the information matrix as the source of the asymptotic standard errors for their parameter estimates.

### Relationship to Other IRT Models

Two additional points pertain to the RSM's relationships to other IRT models that do not apply directly to the PCM in its usual form as expounded by Masters (1982, 1988a; Masters & Wright, 1984, 1997). Both points follow from the fact that the RSM was developed using a scoring function formulation. The first point is that the RSM is directly and explicitly related to Rasch's (1961) polytomous model, whereas the PCM is not. The earlier discussion of how the PCM (Equation 3.5) can be developed to become the RSM (Equation 3.10) suggests, however, that the PCM's separation from Rasch's model is somewhat artificial.

Second, the scoring function formulation of the RSM makes more obvious the connection between the polytomous Rasch models and the NRM. The connection is simply that if the scoring function is considered to be a set of estimable parameters that need not be ordered, this is the NRM. That is, estimating a separate discrimination parameter for each item category and allowing those parameters to be unordered describes the process for obtaining parameters for nominal item categories. This is not as clear when discussing the RSM scoring function because the RSM requires ordered thresholds as a part of its modeling of ordered categories. Recall that the PCM does not require ordered category boundaries. Thus, the notion of nominalizing response categories might be more intuitively obvious in the context of a scoring function formulation of the PCM.

## PCM Scoring Function Formulation and the NRM

Andrich (1988a) shows how the PCM can be expressed in terms of the scoring function formulation that he uses for the RSM, in a manner that is formally equivalent to Muraki's GPCM approach, which will be described in more detail in the next section. He shows that the PCM is simply Equation 3.10 with the $\tau_{i_g}$ allowed to vary across items, and therefore estimated separately for each item rather than once, as a set, for all items in a test. This leads Andrich (1988a) to relabel the PCM as the extended logistic model (ELM).[2] It also shows that just as the RSM can be formulated in terms of the usual PCM formulation (Table 3.1), so the PCM can be formulated in terms of a scoring function and category coefficients, where the category boundaries are defined with respect to a single item location for each item. Andrich also makes the important point that simply reformulating the PCM CBRFs in terms of thresholds does not change the fact that these locations cannot be considered separately but must be considered together, within an item.

Aside from requiring the $\tau_{i_g}$ to be estimated separately for each item, Andrich's (1988a) ELM differs from the RSM in that it does not require the $\tau_g$ to be ordered. Andrich (1988a) does, however, make a convincing argument for the need to avoid reversed category boundaries in ordered polytomous models, irrespective of whether they are in $b_{i_g}$ or $\tau_{i_g}$ form.

The scoring function equivalent of the PCM shown in Equation 3.1 is therefore simply

$$P_{i_g} = \frac{e^{[\kappa_{i_g} + \phi_g(\theta - b_i)]}}{\sum_{h=0}^{m} e^{[\kappa_{i_h} + \phi_h(\theta - b_i)]}}, \qquad (3.23)$$

where

$$\kappa_{i_g} = -\sum_{g=0}^{l} \tau_{i_g}, \qquad (3.24)$$

with $\tau_{i_g}$ now estimated separately for each item and need not be ordered, and where $\phi_g$ is the usual linear integer scoring function.

If the threshold discrimination parameters $a_g$ are estimated rather than being stipulated equal to 1.0, and are also allowed to be unordered, Equation 3.23 becomes

$$P_{i_g} = \frac{e^{[\kappa_{i_g} + \phi_{i_g}(\theta - b_i)]}}{\sum_{h=0}^{m} e^{[\kappa_{i_h} + \phi_{i_h}(\theta - b_i)]}}, \quad (3.25)$$

now with

$$\kappa_{i_g} = -\sum_{g=0}^{l} a_{i_g} \tau_{i_g}, \quad (3.26)$$

and

$$\phi_{i_g} = \sum_{g=0}^{l} a_{i_g}. \quad (3.27)$$

Equation 3.25 is the scoring function formulation of the NRM.

Reformulating the PCM in terms of a scoring function, as in Equation 3.23, also allows Andrich (1988a) to explore a key difference between dichotomous and polytomous Rasch models. He notes that although the dichotomous Rasch model IRFs are constrained to have the same discrimination, this need not be the case for PCM (or RSM) IRFs. Appreciating this difference requires understanding the earlier discussion on how an IRF is obtained for a polytomous item by means of the expected score. The reason the difference exists is that the "distances" between the thresholds, for items modeled by both the PCM and RSM, affect the items' discrimination. The further apart the $\tau_{i_g}$ values, when the thresholds are in the same order as the item categories, the weaker the discrimination. The converse is also true, as is the fact that when thresholds are reversed, the item discriminates even more sharply than for naturally ordered categories (Andrich, 1988a). This description of discrimination echoes Muraki's (1992) comment that the discrimination of a polytomous item is composed of the item's slope parameter and the set of threshold parameters for the item.

The key difference between dichotomous and polytomous Rasch models, described by Andrich (1988a), therefore centers on the respective item location parameters. A dichotomous item response allows the estimation of only a single location parameter. In contrast, when a subset of dichotomous items, such as a testlet, or when a polytomous item is being modeled by the PCM, it becomes possible to estimate a location and the distance between two items' or two categories' thresholds. An implication of this distinction is that dichotomous IRT models that allow discrimination to vary from item to item (e.g., 2PL) may be masking item dependencies in a test (e.g., see Masters, 1988b), with the associated risks that follow from a breakdown of the local independence assumption.

## Variations

### Andrich Elaborations

A number of variations of the RSM are possible by virtue of the fact that the relationships among thresholds can be constrained in different ways, both within and across items. Andrich (1978b), in his original explication of the RSM, showed how to modify the RSM so that all thresholds are the same distance apart. The important point he made there was that equidistant thresholds were a function of the form of the category coefficients and not due to the integer scoring function. Andrich (1982) generalized this early demonstration model by showing that it resulted from adding a dispersion parameter to the formulation of the category coefficient. This dispersion parameter can be estimated easily, and although it results in equal distances, it need not result in unit distances between thresholds. The important role of this dispersion parameter—together with the fact that thresholds are defined, in the usual RSM manner, relative to a central item location parameter—lead Andrich to refer to this as the dispersion, location model (DLM).

Andrich (1982) also showed that the DLM can be applied in two distinct ways. If one retains the rating scale assumption that all rating items in a test should function in the same manner, then only one dispersion parameter value need be estimated for an entire test. The result is that the distance between all the thresholds within an item would be modeled to be the same, and this distance would also apply across all items in a test. In other words, the size of every category within and across items using a specific rating scale would be the same, although they would not necessarily be one scale unit in size. This could be called a rating scale version of the DLM (RS-DLM).

The second way to apply the DLM is to estimate a separate dispersion parameter for every item in a test. In this case, all categories within an item are modeled to be the same size, but the category size can vary across items. Although this variation can still apply to items that have the same number of categories, the rating scale assumption clearly no longer holds because categories are no longer functioning in the same way across items. Andrich (1982) notes that the DLM variations that allow category size to vary across items require items with at least three ordered categories. The dispersion parameter cannot be constructed for a dichotomous response.

The algebraic form of the DLM clearly shows the role of the dispersion parameter. This is

$$P_{i_g} = \frac{e^{[\phi_g(\theta-b_i)+g(m-g)\lambda_i]}}{\sum_{g=0}^{m} e^{[\phi_g(\theta-b_i)+g(m-g)\lambda_i]}}, \tag{3.28}$$

where the quadratic function $g(m - g)$ multiplied by the dispersion parameter $\lambda_i$ replaces the usual RSM form of the category coefficients $\kappa_g$. Note that when a single dispersion parameter is estimated for an entire dataset, the subscript $i$ is not required on $\lambda$.

Obtaining threshold $(\tau_{i_g})$ values from the DLM is different from the case of the RSM, where threshold values are obtained simply by subtracting successive category coefficient values such that

$$\tau_g = \kappa_{g-1} - \kappa_g \tag{3.29}$$

with

$$\tau_1 = 0 - \kappa_1. \tag{3.30}$$

The process differs for the DLM because the category coefficient component is no longer simply a sum of thresholds. Instead, Müller (1987) shows that DLM threshold values can be obtained from the simple formula

$$\tau_{i_g} = 2\lambda_i \left( g - \frac{m+1}{2} \right). \tag{3.31}$$

Andrich (1982) shows that the dispersion parameter $(\lambda_g)$ of the DLM can indicate the plausibility of the response distribution for an item. This essentially provides an assessment of model plausibility and follows directly from the value of $\lambda_i$. If the dispersion parameter is greater than zero, the response distribution is unimodal and suggests a plausible response process. If it equals zero, then responses are distributed uniformly and response dependencies are implied (Andrich, 1985b). However, if the dispersion parameter's value is below zero, the response distribution is U-shaped, suggesting that the model does not fit the response data. A negative dispersion parameter is directly related to the issue of reversed category boundaries, which Andrich (1988a) argues is problematic and which contravenes a basic requirement of the rating models elaborated by Andrich.

Andrich (1985a) introduces the idea that additional parameters can be incorporated into the DLM to describe more aspects of category structure. Specifically, he introduces a third item parameter, $\eta_i$, that indexes skew. This parameter can be interpreted as characterizing response set when applied to questionnaire data and is called an asymmetry parameter (Andrich, 1985a).

The skew parameter is, logically, scored by a cubic function such that the category coefficients, $\kappa_g$, of the RSM now take the form

$$\kappa_g = g(m - g)\lambda_i + g(m - g)(2g - m)\eta_i. \qquad (3.32)$$

## Rost Elaborations

Rost (1988a) developed a model that attempts to address the original concerns of Thurstone's method of successive intervals (Edwards & Thurstone, 1952; Rimoldi & Hormaeche, 1955), which he identifies as a need to scale category widths while allowing category boundaries to be dispersed differently from item to item. Rost notes that the RSM scales category boundaries, whereas the DLM addresses variable boundary dispersions, but neither accommodates both factors.

Rost's (1988a) solution is to develop the successive intervals model (SIM) by combining the RSM and DLM approaches. That is, a set of thresholds is estimated for the entire set of data from a given rating scale (as per RSM). Additionally, a dispersion parameter is estimated for each item (as per DLM). Then the final, unique, threshold locations for each item are a combination of these two item parameters. Thus, thresholds are not constant across items, because a unique item dispersion parameter modifies the baseline rating scale condition. Neither are they constant within an item, because the dispersion modification is to RSM-type thresholds, which themselves have variable interval sizes within items. This produces a general model that accommodates varying threshold locations across and within items while still being considerably more parsimonious with regard to the total number of parameters to be estimated than the PCM.

For completeness, it should be noted that Rost's (1988a) SIM is part of a much broader body of work combining latent class analysis with IRT. Through a series of expositions, Rost (1988b, 1988c, 1990, 1991) incorporates increasingly less restricted versions of dichotomous and polytomous Rasch models into the latent class modeling framework. Rasch models were chosen for the IRT component because the approach relies on obtaining the item parameters without reference to the trait distribution (Rost, 1990), and this can be done only if sufficient statistics are available for the parameters. The approach is intriguing because it provides a method for quantitatively measuring people, using Rasch models, within qualitatively different groups, defined as latent classes (Rost, 1991).

### Other Elaborations

A Rasch model for continuous ratings, such as those produced by a graphic rating scale, was developed by Müller (1987). Müller conceived of continuous rating scales as a limiting case of ordered categorical rating scales where the number of categories becomes infinitely large. The continuous model developed by Müller is an elaboration of the DLM outlined by Andrich (1982) and is obtained by using a more general scoring formula than the usual integer scoring function.

Another set of polytomous Rasch models has also been developed in the context of the scoring function formulation used by Rasch (1961) and elaborated by Andrich (1978b). These models were developed by Fischer because there were no appropriate methods for assessing, or testing hypotheses about, treatment effects with ordered polytomous models (Fischer & Ponocny, 1994, 1995).

The approach taken in this set of models is to decompose the item parameters into linear components called basic parameters. The basic parameters are defined generally enough that they can represent any experimental factor or structural property of an item that is expected to influence the item's trait scale location (Fischer & Parzer, 1991; Fischer & Ponocny, 1994). Thus, they can represent, for example, cognitive operations involved in responding to an item, the effect of some treatment or of learning on a trait, or the effect of advertising or some other communication on an attitude (Fischer & Ponocny, 1994).

## Generalized Partial Credit Model

In the previous section, some RSM variations were described that resulted from constraining threshold relationships in different ways. An alternative is to take advantage of Andrich's introduction of a discrimination parameter in Equation 3.6 and develop variations of the RSM by allowing this parameter to vary across items. This has important implications for the status of the resulting models as Rasch models.

The major variant of the RSM that takes advantage of a discrimination parameter that varies across items is the GPCM, which was introduced briefly in the earlier section on PCM variants. The place of Muraki's (1992) GPCM as a variant not only of the PCM (Masters, 1982) but also of the RSM (Andrich, 1978b) is demonstrated by Muraki's (1997) representation of the GPCM in terms of the scoring function formulation of polytomous Rasch models that is used by Andrich.

The equation for this formulation of the GPCM is

$$p_{i_g} = \frac{e^{a_i\left[\phi_g(\theta-b_i)+\sum_{g=1}^l \tau_g\right]}}{\sum_{h=1}^m e^{a_i\left[\phi_h(\theta-b_i)+\sum_{g=1}^h \tau_g\right]}}, \tag{3.33}$$

where

$a_i$ is the slope parameter representing item discrimination (one per item);

$b_i$ is the item location parameter (one per item);

$\phi_i$ is the usual scoring function (defined here as a scaling factor) that equals the category count for the specific category ($g$) being modeled; and $\tau_{i_g}$ is the threshold parameter representing the category boundary locations relative to the item location parameter .

Note that Muraki does not represent GPCM-summed thresholds as a category coefficient ($\kappa_{i_g}$) the way Andrich does for the RSM.

Muraki (1997) argues that allowing nonuniform discrimination across all items in a test means that the GPCM allows more insight into the characteristics of the test items than does the PCM. An important attraction of the GPCM is that the twin tactics of adding an item discrimination parameter and employing the scoring function formulation to describe the model make it a flexible framework for describing a wide range of polytomous IRT models. All of the potential models are, of course, divide-by-total models in Thissen and Steinberg's (1986) terminology. Nevertheless, by constraining the discrimination ($a_i$), scoring function ($\phi_g$), and threshold ($\tau_{i_g}$) parameters of test items in different ways, a collection of IRT models can be described. This strategy also can help illuminate some of the relationships among different models as well as further demonstrate some of the enormous flexibility of the polytomous item format. Some examples of this strategy are described below.

In Equation 3.33, when the slope parameter ($a_i$) is fixed equal to 1.0 and a set of threshold parameters ($\tau_{i_g}$) is estimated separately for each item, with the additional condition that these parameters need not be ordered on $\theta$, this becomes the scoring function formulation of the equation for the PCM (Masters, 1982). This is also identical to the ELM described by Andrich (1988a).

When the $a_i$ are free to vary across items, but the $\tau_g$ are constrained to be ordered according to the item category ordering and are estimated once for all items in a set of items, then Equation 3.33 becomes the RSM (Andrich, 1978b) with a varying slope parameter—in a sense, a generalized rating scale model.

A systematic listing of these model variations is provided in Table 3.2, which replicates the intent of Table 3.1 from the beginning of the section on polytomous Rasch models. That is, it shows how different models can be obtained from a single general model. In this case, however, it does so using the scoring function formulation of the various models based on Muraki's (1992) general equation (Equation 3.33) above. This formulation allows non-Rasch models to also be included in this pseudo-taxonomy.

TABLE 3.2

The Scoring Function Formulation
Context of Some Ordered IRT Models

Probability of responding in category $g$ of item $i$, conditional on $\theta$, is,

$$P_{i_g} = \frac{e^{a_i\left[\phi_g(\theta-b_i)+\sum_{g=1}^{l}\tau_{ig}\right]}}{\sum_{h=1}^{m} e^{a_i\left[\phi_h(\theta-b_i)+\sum_{g=1}^{h}\tau_{ig}\right]}},$$

where

$a_i$ is the slope parameter; represents item discrimination;

$b_i$ is the item location parameter;

$\tau_{i_g}$ are the category threshold parameters;

$\phi_h$ is the scoring function; typically a linear function with elements equal to the category numbers; and

$h = 0, 1, \ldots, g, \ldots, m$ item categories, with $g$ representing the category being modeled.

When $a_i$ is estimated and varies across items,

$\tau_{i_g}$ are not constrained to follow item category ordering, and

$\tau_{i_g}$ are estimated separately for each item,

this is the generalized partial credit model.

When $a_i$ is fixed = 1, and

$\tau_{i_g}$ are as in the GPCM,

this is the partial credit model.

When $a_i$ is fixed =1,

$\tau_g$ are constrained to follow category ordering, and

$\tau_g$ are estimated once for an entire set of items,

this is the rating scale model.

When $a_i$ is estimated and varies across items, and

$\tau_{i_g}$ are as in the RSM,

this is a generalized rating scale model.

When $a_i$ is fixed =1,

$\tau_{i_g}$ are as in the GPCM, and

$\phi_h$ may vary from the typical linear function (either fixed based on a priori knowledge, or estimated),

this is the ordered partition model.

When $a_i$ is estimated and varies across items,

and $m + 1 = 2$,

this is the 2-parameter logistic, dichotomous model.

When $a_i$ is fixed = 1, and

$m + 1 = 2$,

this is the dichotomous Rasch model (SLM).

Note: Any time $a_i$ or the $\phi_h$ are estimated and are free to vary across items, the resultant model is not a Rasch model.

It is important to remember that the RSM, the PCM, and, by extension, the GPCM become models for ordered categorical responses only when the scoring function is increasing (Muraki, 1997). This means that it must be the case that $\phi_h > \phi_{h-1}$ for any category $h$ within an item. Furthermore, the discrimination parameter, $a_{i_g}$, must also be greater than 0. If $a_{i_g}$ is allowed to be negative, the categories become nominal and the PCM becomes the NRM (Hemker, 1996).

## Discrimination and Polytomous Rasch Models

By introducing a discrimination parameter, Andrich (1978b) provides a substantive interpretation for the category coefficient $\kappa_g$ and scoring function $\phi_g$ of Rasch's (1961) polytomous model. The interpretation, however, rests on two important points, as Andrich (1978b) makes clear. First, in Rasch models, discrimination is indexed only by threshold, $a_g$, and not by item and threshold, $a_{i_g}$. Second, these threshold discriminations are not estimated, but rather must be a constant so that the scoring function increases by the same amount from category to category. This allows independent, minimally sufficient statistics (Andersen, 1977), and when this constant is set equal to 1.0, the usual linear integer scoring function ensues.

Muraki (1992) reintroduces item discrimination, but now as a separate entity $(a_i)$ rather than in combination with threshold discrimination $(a_{i_g})$. This allows Muraki to retain the linear integer scoring function and its interpretation in terms of threshold discrimination and category scores while providing a means for modeling varying discrimination on an item-by-item basis.

In addition to the separation of item and threshold discrimination, a key issue in the foregoing discussion is whether or not the parameter is estimated. If either the item or threshold parameters are to be estimated, where the former is the case with the GPCM, the resulting model is not a Rasch model. This is because requiring a discrimination parameter to be estimated precludes the possibility of obtaining the sufficient statistics required for parameter separation, in exactly the same manner as with the 2PL model in the dichotomous case. Thus, the GPCM—and similarly, any generalized RSM—are not Rasch models, any more than the NRM, even though they all have the divide-by-total form to their model equations.

## Summary of Polytomous Rasch Models

The polytomous Rasch model strategy of local dichotomizations combined in a divide-by-total framework results in models that are specifically objective. That is, they are objective because two items can be compared independently of which people responded to the items and independently of any other items in a test, and similarly, two people can be compared independently of the items to which they responded and of which other people could be compared (Rasch, 1961). Furthermore, they are specifically objective because the comparisons take place within a specified frame of reference, usually with respect to a specific trait. Specific objectivity is, in practical terms, inextricably linked to the availability of sufficient statistics for the model parameters (Andrich, 1996).

The partial credit model (PCM) and the rating scale model (RSM) are the most prominent manifestations of polytomous Rasch models. Both can be presented in terms of a scoring function formulation, although the PCM was not developed using that formulation. When presented in terms of a scoring function, the PCM is often referred to as the extended logistic model (ELM), reflecting its status as a general model where no restrictions are made on the number of, or relationships among, item categories across items in a test.

Aside from differences in the form of the general equations within which the PCM and RSM were initially presented, and their different levels of generality, the two models also differ in terms of the response process posited to underlie them. It has been suggested that the PCM models a series of sequential dichotomous steps that is represented by the category boundaries, whereas the RSM has been suggested to model the entire set of dichotomous choices represented by the category boundaries simultaneously. Although the RSM process avoids the implication associated with the sequential steps approach that requires each step to incorporate information about what occurs in subsequent steps, it retains the problem of ambiguously defined category boundary location parameters endemic to polytomous Rasch models. This ambiguity arises from the fact that even though category boundaries are locally defined, they occur in the context of a polytomous item, and the location of any given boundary therefore is influenced by the locations of adjacent boundaries, which, in turn, have their locations influenced by the locations of boundaries adjacent to them. It is an interesting irony for polytomous Rasch models that, although they arguably have no plausible response process underlying them (van Engelenburg, 1997), they are the only polytomous IRT models that always result in stochastically ordered trait estimates (Hemker, 1996).

The local dichotomization approach of polytomous Rasch models also results in the situation where category boundary locations need not be in the same order on the trait continuum as the categories they separate. This has sometimes been described as a strength of the polytomous Rasch models, particularly in contrast to the Thurstone/Samejima approach (Masters, 1982), or at least as perfectly understandable (Adams, 1988). Boundary reversals, however, may not actually be desirable.

For example, Andrich (1988a) notes that whenever category boundaries are reversed, there will be one or more categories that are never the most probable. So, although reversed boundaries might be used as a diagnostic tool to help provide understanding of the cognitive processes at work in responding to an item, they probably indicate that something is wrong with the item (Andrich, 1988a). Verhelst, Glas, and de Vries (1997), however, suggest that, given the ambiguous nature of the boundary location parameters in polytomous Rasch models, they are, in fact, unhelpful for diagnostic purposes.

This chapter on polytomous Rasch models began by introducing the PCM as a potential model for a large range of polytomous item types in the social sciences, including those used in personality, cognitive, and attitude measurement. It can also apply to nonindependent dichotomous item sets such as those used in item bundles and testlets. Furthermore, the model accommodates items with different numbers of categories. Discussion then turned to the possibility of modifying the PCM by allowing discrimination to vary, which in one case leads to the GPCM. Variations of the PCM were also introduced, which, in one case, allowed the modeling of null categories and, in another, the inclusion of multiple, nominal categories within an ordered polytomous item (i.e., the OPM).

Introduction of the RSM was notable because it provides an alternative response rationale to the contentious steps notion associated with the PCM, and because it elaborates an alternative parameterization of Rasch models, namely, the scoring function formulation. This formulation helps clarify the sources of polytomous Rasch model flexibility, specifically in terms of the scoring function and category coefficient parameters. It also highlights the context in which simple sufficient statistics for model parameters arise.

By reformulating the PCM in its scoring function formulation as the ELM, it was shown that different models could be obtained by constraining the thresholds in different ways through alternate definitions of the category coefficient. This led to such models as the "classic" RSM, as well as the DLM, the DSLM, and the SIM.

Perhaps more importantly, the scoring function formulation of Rasch models makes more obvious the fact that discrimination can occur at an item level or at a category boundary level in polytomous items. Elaborating the role of the scoring function in discrimination helped clarify such issues as the link between the NRM and the polytomous Rasch models, and the prerequisites needed for sufficient statistics to be available, particularly through the work of Andersen (1977, 1983).

The flexibility in polytomous Rasch models is enhanced by the technique of decomposing item location parameters into—once again, predetermined—linear composites, as in the linear logistic models of Fischer (Fischer & Parzer, 1991; Fisher & Ponocny, 1994, 1995). Rost's (1988b, 1988c, 1990, 1991) work integrating latent class analysis with individual differences measurement by means of polytomous Rasch models is another example of the flexibility of the basic Rasch approach.

## Three Practical Examples

The remaining practical examples (PCM, RSM, GPCM, and, in the next chapter, the GRM) will all use the same data in order to highlight similarities and differences in the four models in the context of a common set of data. The data come from a survey of people's notions of morality that obtained responses using a 5-point Likert-type rating scale. Screening of the initial survey data resulted in a final set of 999 responses to 93 items. Responses were primarily obtained from students at a large midwestern university. A dimensionality analysis of these data produced a 12-factor principal axis factor analysis solution that was rotated by varimax rotation. Twelve items were identified as loading on the first factor of this 12-factor solution. This set of 12 items was selected for IRT analysis because it represents the strongest single construct dimension of the full dataset.

The items in this dataset contained responses in every response category. Category response frequencies ranged from a minimum of 24 to a maximum of 397. IRT analysis was conducted using Parscale (Muraki & Bock, 1999) for all of the practical examples using these data. This reduces the prospect of model variation due to variation in software parameter estimation routines. Item 4 was selected from the 12 items in this first dimension for use in the practical examples, primarily because it was located in the middle of the trait range, thus enhancing the presentation of the response functions.

### PCM

Only one item parameter $(b_{i_g})$ is estimated in the PCM. However, this boundary location parameter must be estimated separately for each boundary of every item in a test or questionnaire. Note that in the adjacent category models, the category boundary parameter values need not be ordered in the same sequence as are the categories, because adjacent category boundaries involve local dichotomizations. However, when boundaries are out of order, this indicates that at least one item category will never be the most probable response for respondents at any point on the trait scale. It is also considered an indication of an item that is not functioning as intended (Andrich, 1988a). As we discuss specific parameter values, it is also important to remember from the earlier "Item Steps" discussion that

TABLE 3.3

Parameter Values for a Morality Item Using the Partial Credit
Model, the Rating Scale Model, and the Generalized Partial Credit Model

| Model | | 1 | 2 | 3 | 4 |
|---|---|---|---|---|---|
| PCM | $b_{i_g}$ | −1.618 | − 0.291 | 0.414 | 2.044 |
| RSM | $b_i = 0.155$ | | | | |
| | $\tau_g$ | −1.388 | − 0.610 | 0.316 | 1.682 |
| | $b_{i_g} = b_i + \tau_g$ | −1.233 | − 0.455 | 0.471 | 1.837 |
| GPCM | $a_i = 0.395$ | | | | |
| | $b_{i_g}$ | −3.419 | − 0.482 | 0.777 | 4.240 |

adjacent category models $b_{i_g}$ do not actually model independent boundary locations, trait levels, or "difficulties" because the local boundary dichotomizations occur in the context of an entire item. Discussion of category boundary locations below therefore refers to nonindependent item parameters.

Table 3.3 contains the four $b_{i_g}$ values that describe the PCM (nonindependent) CBRF locations for our example item. Note that for this item, the boundaries are sequentially ordered, indicating a well-functioning item. The ICRFs for this item are shown in Figure 3.2. This figure shows that all five categories have some segment of the trait scale along which a response in the respective categories is more probable than for any other category. The category with the shortest such segment is Category 3. In practice, the middle category in Likert-type items with odd numbers of categories is the category that most commonly is found to be "never most probable." This occurrence may be an indication that the middle category is being used by respondents as a "Don't Know" or "Can't Decide" category instead of operating as a legitimate measure of the middle part of the trait continuum for an item.

The middle category of the example item may be demonstrating some effects of responses that are not legitimately trait-indicating, because its ICRF's peak is lower than those of adjacent categories. However, it is also legitimately measuring the middle of the trait continuum for some respondents. This is suggested by the fact that it is the most probable response category for respondents with $-0.250 < \theta < 0.375$. For respondents in the region of the trait continuum immediately below $\theta = -0.250$, a response in Category 2 becomes most probable, whereas immediately above $\theta = 0.375$, a Category 4 response becomes most probable.

To facilitate comparisons across models, specific response probabilities are provided in Table 3.4, for each item category, at two arbitrary points

58

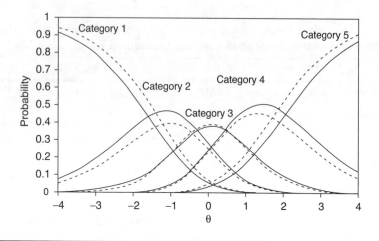

**Figure 3.2**    ICRFs for a Likert-Type Morality Item Modeled by the PCM and RSM

Key: Solid line = PCM; dashed line = RSM.

on the trait continuum ($\theta = -1.5$ and $\theta = 1.5$). Table 3.4 shows that, as modeled by the PCM, respondents at $\theta = -1.5$ have the highest probability of responding in Category 2, whereas Category 5 is the most probable response category for those at $\theta = 1.5$.

### RSM

Two types of item parameters are estimated for the RSM. Table 3.3 shows the relevant item location ($b_i$) and threshold location ($\tau_g$) parameters for our example item. A total of five parameters have been estimated for this item, in contrast to only four $b_{i_g}$ parameters for the PCM. Recall, however, that the set of four $\tau_g$ shown here is estimated only once for all 12 of the items in the questionnaire dimension from which this example item was taken, and only the $b_i$ parameter is estimated separately for each item. In general, the total number of RSM parameters for an $n$-length test with $m$ categories is $n + (m - 1)$. Except for very short tests, this will always be fewer than the $n(m - 1)$ PCM parameters that must be estimated for a test.

To obtain specific category boundary locations for an item, it is necessary to combine an item's unique location parameter with the testwide common threshold parameters (see Figure 3.1). The result of this process for our example item is shown in Table 3.3. Note that although the resulting boundary locations are similar to the PCM locations, all of the RSM

TABLE 3.4

Response Probabilities for a Morality Item Across Three Adjacent
Category Models, at Two Points on the Trait Scale

| | | \multicolumn{5}{c}{Item Category} | | | |
|---|---|---|---|---|---|---|
| Model | | 1 | 2 | 3 | 4 | 5 |
| PCM | $p\|\theta = -1.5$ | 0.398 | 0.448 | 0.134 | 0.020 | 0.001 |
| | $p\|\theta = 1.5$ | 0.001 | 0.028 | 0.171 | 0.506 | 0.294 |
| RSM | $p\|\theta = -1.5$ | 0.482 | 0.369 | 0.130 | 0.018 | 0.001 |
| | $p\|\theta = 1.5$ | 0.001 | 0.022 | 0.159 | 0.445 | 0.371 |
| GPCM | $p\|\theta = -1.5$ | 0.192 | 0.410 | 0.274 | 0.112 | 0.012 |
| | $p\|\theta = 1.5$ | 0.020 | 0.138 | 0.303 | 0.403 | 0.136 |

boundary locations do differ from the PCM locations for the same item. In particular, the range of the trait scale covered by the boundaries (from $b_{i_1}$ to $b_{i_4}$) is smaller for the RSM than it is for the PCM.

This outcome is reflected in the RSM ICRFs, shown as dashed lines in Figure 3.2. The PCM and RSM ICRFs are shown in the same figure to facilitate comparisons. For example, the smaller trait continuum range covered by the RSM boundaries is clearly evident in a comparison of RSM and PCM ICRFs for Categories 1 and 5. This narrowing of the trait range for this item also has consequences for Category 2 and Category 4 ICRFs, which, for the RSM, have lower maxima than the PCM ICRFs for these two categories. The ICRFs for Category 3 are, however, very similar across the two models.

The effect of the different ICRFs for the two models is shown in Table 3.4. It shows that at $\theta = -1.5$, Category 1 is the most probable response as modeled by the RSM rather than Category 2 at this trait level for the PCM. At $\theta = 1.5$, Category 4 is the most probable response as modeled by both the RSM and the PCM. However, the probability of responding in this category (for respondents at this trait level) is lower for the RSM than was modeled by the PCM.

### GPCM

Five parameters unique to each item must be estimated for the GPCM. The single-item discrimination and four category boundary location parameters unique to our example item are shown in Table 3.3. Note that the estimated GPCM item discrimination for this item ($a_i = 0.395$) is considerably lower than the implied, but not estimated, PCM and RSM item discrimination, which is $a_i = 1.0$.

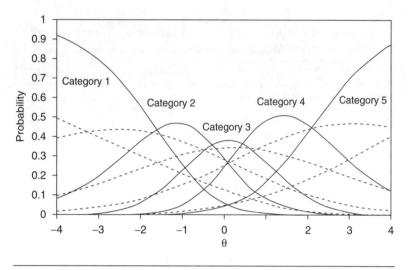

**Figure 3.3**    ICRFs for a Likert-Type Morality Item Modeled by the PCM and GPCM

Key: Solid line = PCM; dashed line = GPCM.

Previously, with the RSM, the application of a testwide set of category thresholds to our example item resulted in a contraction of the range of the trait continuum measured by this item, compared to the range measured using the PCM-modeled parameters. In contrast, estimating a discrimination parameter for the example item has contributed to a more than doubling of the trait continuum range between the first and last category boundaries for the GPCM, compared to the same boundary parameters for the PCM. This is demonstrated in the ICRFs shown in Figure 3.3, where the GPCM functions are noticeably flatter, and the range of most probable responding is wider, for each category when compared to the PCM ICRFs for this item.

It is interesting to note that the flattening of the category response functions has not affected which are the most probable response categories for this item at $\theta = -1.5$ and $\theta = 1.5$, respectively, when modeled by the GPCM compared to the PCM (see Table 3.4). Response probabilities are, however, lower for the GPCM modeled most probable categories at both of the $\theta$ levels shown relative to the PCM response probabilities. The flattening of the GPCM ICRFs however, also means that the probability of responding in Category 3 is higher at both $\theta = -1.5$ and $\theta = 1.5$ as modeled by the GPCM compared to the PCM. This is made quite clear in Figure 3.3.

## 4. SAMEJIMA MODELS

The only major approach to polytomous IRT modeling that is distinct from the Rasch-type models is the work of Samejima, which is built on the cumulative boundary measurement approach of Thurstone. Samejima (1969) initially developed two such models designed to allow researchers to estimate respondents' standing on a trait from their responses to a set of items with an ordered polytomous response format. Much of this work focused on maximum likelihood estimation for the person (trait) parameter. The two models had an identical form and differed only in that one employed a normal ogive to model responses, and ultimately to construct an item's ICRFs, whereas the second used a logistic function for this purpose. Samejima (1972) later expanded and formalized the basic framework of her earlier work to accommodate free-response data that could conceivably include a potentially unlimited number of unordered responses to a test item.

Samejima provides a limited number of practical measurement models for specific situations. Unfortunately, in the literature, there is often a failure to differentiate a specific practical model, by name, from the general class of models to which it belongs. This has led to some confusion in labeling and understanding Samejima's framework and the constituent, specific models.

### Framework

Table 4.1 presents a way to think of Samejima's theoretical framework. Working from left to right, we begin with specific data types. These can be specialized from free-response data either at the outset by the format of the data collection, or by subsequent, valid ordering or categorization procedures. Of course, in many practical testing situations, the data will, in fact, be collected in a format corresponding to one of the more specific types.

Samejima (1972, 1997b) describes what are essentially two broad theoretical classes of models that can be used to model the specific data types listed in the first column. The two classes of models are referred to as the heterogeneous and the homogeneous cases, and the appropriate class for each data type is listed in the second column of the table. The most interesting feature to note here is that ordered, polytomous data can be modeled by either the heterogeneous or homogeneous classes of models. Nominal data, however, can be modeled only by the heterogeneous class of models (Samejima, 1972).

The final column lists specific models that have been developed over time, with respect to the general class of models to which they belong and, by extension, the specific data types to which they explicitly apply. Two other interesting points highlighted in this final column are that not all

TABLE 4.1
Samejima's General Framework for Polytomous Data

| More specific polytomous data types | which can be modeled by → | General classes of models | using → | Specific models |
|---|---|---|---|---|
| *Theoretical Framework* | | | | |
| Continuous nominal (e.g., ungrouped Rorschach data) | | Heterogeneous (continuous) | | None |
| Continuous ordered (e.g., graphic rating scales) | | Heterogeneous (continuous) Homogeneous (continuous) | | Continuous Rasch model (Müller, 1987) Continuous response model (Samejima, 1973) |
| Discrete nominal (e.g., multiple-choice test items) | | Heterogeneous (categorical) | | Nominal response model (Bock, 1972) |
| Discrete ordered (e.g., rating scale items) | | Heterogeneous (categorical) | | Acceleration model (Samejima, 1995); Polytomous Rasch models; Generalized partial credit models (per Muraki, 1992) |
| | | Homogeneous (categorical) | | Graded response models (Samejima, 1969) |

of the specific models have been developed by Samejima herself, and that in some cases, a number of applicable models are potentially available for use.

The lack of a clear distinction between the theoretical framework and the specific models is probably due to the fact that the specific models developed by Samejima grow directly out of the underlying framework. That framework is tied directly to the response processes hypothesized to generate the various types of response data.

This is an important difference between Samejima's models and the polytomous Rasch models. As has been mentioned numerous times, the Rasch models are built on the requirement of model parameter separability, with the associated issues of sufficiency, specific objectivity, and fundamental measurement. Any hypothesized response process that may have generated the data to be modeled is essentially an afterthought.

In Samejima's framework, however, the plausibility of the response process thought to generate data is paramount, because for Samejima (1979a), the main role of a mathematical model in psychology is to plausibly represent psychological reality. Thus, the hypothetical response process is not ancillary speculation, as it tends to be for the Rasch models; rather, it is the foundation for her whole approach to modeling polytomous data. Any discussion of Samejima's work therefore must begin with her interpretation of a realistic underlying psychological reality and proceed by showing the bridge to specific models.

## From Response Process to Specific Model

The response process hypothesized by Samejima (1972) to underlie the specific models in her framework is built on the notion that each response category of an item exerts a level of attraction on individuals. By implication, this attraction varies across individuals who vary in trait level, and is a function of $\theta$. This attraction toward a category is also defined contingent on the person having already been attracted by the previous category. The function describing the probability of being attracted to a particular category $g$, over and above an attraction to the previous category, $g - 1$, is designated $M_{i_g}(\theta)$. Samejima (1995, 1997b) calls this the *processing function.*

In the context of an entire item, then, being attracted to a category must take all prior category attractions into account. This can be expressed as the serial product of the attractions to each successive category, over and above the attraction to the respective prior categories. Competing with this attraction for any given category is the further attraction of the next category. The probability of being attracted to the next category can be designated $M_{i_{g+1}}(\theta)$. This can also be thought of as the probability of rejecting the previous category. In those terms, the probability is designated $U_{i_g}(\theta)$. Naturally, this implies that the value of $M_{i_g}$ is also the probability of rejecting category $g - 1$.

Given this web of competing attractions (and rejections), the probability of responding in any given category is simply a combination of being attracted through all previous categories up to the given category, but then no further; that is, the probability of the serial attraction up to the category multiplied by the probability of not rejecting that category.

In the case of ordered categories, this process assumes that to respond in a particular category, a person must have passed through all preceding categories (Samejima, 1972). The psychological process being postulated is therefore a cumulative process of successively accepting and then rejecting categories, where rejecting a category is defined as being more attracted to the next category, until a category is reached where the probability of attraction is greater than the probability of rejection.

The cumulative attraction is operationalized as $P^*_{i_g}(\theta)$, where $P^*_{i_g}$ is defined as the probability of responding positively at a category boundary given all previous categories, conditional on $\theta$. As we saw earlier, the probability of responding in a category can then simply be calculated as the probability of responding positively at a category boundary minus the probability of responding positively at the next category boundary:

$$P_{i_g} = P^*_{i_g} - P^*_{i_{g+1}}. \tag{1.2}$$

Thus, the probability of responding in a particular category is modeled, logically, as the difference between the cumulative probabilities of serial attraction to two adjacent categories. This obviates the need for estimating the probability of rejecting a given category, $U_{i_g}$, or for estimating the component $M_{i_g}$.

We will now look at specific models in terms of the two broad theoretical classes of models that Samejima introduced, that is, the homogeneous case and the heterogeneous case.

## The Homogeneous Case: Graded Response Models

Models that fall within the classification of a homogeneous case of a polytomous model have two notable elements. The first is that they are the only models actually operationalized in terms of Equation 1.2. The second notable feature is that homogeneous models have $P^*_{i_g}$, which are all the same shape within an item (Samejima, 1995, 1997b). This latter feature is the distinguishing theoretical feature of the homogeneous case and gives rise to its title.

Before we turn to the mathematical representation of these models, however, a note about nomenclature is in order. In keeping with what amounts to almost universal usage in the literature, the term *graded response model* (GRM), used in isolation, will refer here only to the logistic example of Samejima's (1969) original two models. The normal ogive example of the original two models will be referred to as the normal ogive version of the GRM. Any references to other specific models will use the specific names that are commonly connected with them. In keeping with standard usage, the terms homogeneous or heterogeneous "class" or "case" will imply a theoretical level of discussion rather than an operationalized model.

**The Mathematical Model**

As a practical application within Samejima's general framework, the GRM is the archetypal model in the framework, in part because it is one of the original models. It is also the polytomous IRT manifestation of Thurstone's method of successive intervals (Burros, 1955; Edwards & Thurstone, 1952; Rimoldi & Hormaeche, 1955) in terms of its structural attributes (e.g., see Andrich, 1995; Masters, 1982; Reiser, 1981; Tutz, 1990), where those attributes are described in the top half of Figure 1.4. As is often noted in the applied literature (e.g., Cooke & Michie, 1997; Flannery, Reise, & Widaman, 1995; Fraley, Waller, & Brennan, 2000; Samejima, 1997b), the GRM is built on the two-parameter logistic (2PL) model because this dichotomous model is used as the function to obtain the cumulative boundary functions denoted by $P^*_{i_g}$. Theoretically, however, the $P^*_{i_g}$ could be represented by any appropriate mathematical function (Samejima, 1972, 1996). In practice, they have only ever been modeled by two types of function, the ubiquitous 2PL, as in the GRM, and the 2-parameter normal ogive dichotomous model, in the generally ignored normal ogive version of the GRM. As mentioned above, both of these versions of the GRM were outlined in Samejima's (1969) seminal work.

The usual equation for a GRM CBRF is

$$P^*_{i_g} = \frac{e^{a_i(\theta - b_{i_g})}}{1 + e^{a_i(\theta - b_{i_g})}},\qquad(4.1)$$

where $a_i$ is the item discrimination parameter and $b_{i_g}$ is the boundary location parameter.

Given this definition of the CBRFs, the GRM arises directly from Equation 1.2. This gives the probability of responding in category $g$ as the difference between the probabilities of responding in or above category $g$ (i.e., $P^*_{i_g}$) and responding in or above category $g + 1$ (i.e., $P^*_{i_{g+1}}$). These $P^*_{i_g}$ were described earlier as Thurstone/Samejima CBRFs, and that is the role they play here.

For Equation 1.2 to completely define an item's ICRFs in terms of the available boundary functions, two additional definitions are required. The first is that the probability of responding in or above the lowest possible category for any item is defined as 1.0, across the entire range of $\theta$. This is operationalized by postulating a boundary below the lowest category, where that boundary is designated $P^*_0(\theta)$ and is located at $-\infty$. Therefore, algebraically,

$$P_0^* = 1, \tag{4.2}$$

and the ICRF for the first category $(P_1^*)$ of any item becomes a monotonically decreasing function defined by Equation 1.2 as $P_0^* - P_1^*$, which is equal to $1 - P_1^*$.

The probability of responding in a category higher than the highest category available, designated $P_{m+1}^*(\theta)$, is defined to equal zero throughout the trait range. Algebraically,

$$P_{m+1}^* = 0, \tag{4.3}$$

which means that the probability of responding in the highest category $(P_{i_m}^*)$ equals the probability of responding positively at the highest category boundary $(P_{i_m}^*)$, because $P_{i_m} = P_{i_m}^* - 0$ by Equation 1.2.

This general approach to parameterizing ordered polytomous items has several relevant features. One is that, unlike the polytomous Rasch models, there is no general model for GRM ICRFs. Each ICRF is modeled separately by Equation 1.2. Furthermore, boundary locations are defined at the inflection point of the CBRFs, that is, the point on the trait continuum where $p = .5$. This also contrasts with polytomous Rasch models where boundary locations are defined at the crossing points of adjacent ICRFs. With the GRM, these ICRF crossing points need not be where the CBRF $p = .5$. A related result is that boundary reversals do not occur in the GRM by virtue of the definition of the boundaries as cumulative probability functions. This set of features accounts for the fact that it is common to see GRM CBRFs plotted explicitly, whereas it is not common to see polytomous Rasch model CBRFs plotted.

By definition, the cumulative CBRFs within items in models that belong to the homogeneous case of Samejima's (1972) framework are all the same shape. This is true whether they are modeled by the 2PL model, as in the GRM, or by the 2-parameter normal ogive, or are any other shaped functions (Samejima, 1996). In the case of the GRM, this effectively translates to mean that, within an item, the CBRFs have the same discrimination. Unlike polytomous Rasch models, category boundary discriminations cannot vary in the GRM, even if they are specified a priori and not estimated. Also unlike the Rasch models, but in a manner analogous to the GPCM, the GRM can model items with discrimination that varies across items.

## Information

Beginning at the broadest level, test information is defined as the negative expectation of the second derivative of the log of the likelihood function of the person parameter θ (Hambleton & Swaminathan, 1985). Algebraically,

$$I(\theta) = -E\left[\frac{\partial^2 \ln L}{\partial \theta^2}\right], \qquad (4.4)$$

where $I(\theta)$ denotes test information, conditional on θ, and $L$ represents the likelihood function of a test. Of course, this always results in a positive value because the second derivative of the log of the likelihood function itself is always negative.

Test information, however, is also defined in terms of the sum of item information for the items in a test, assessed across the range of θ. We know that item information equals the squared IRF slope divided by conditional variance, from earlier discussions of information, where the first derivative of the IRF is indicative of slope. Furthermore, in the dichotomous case, the probability of a positive response ($P_i$) multiplied by the probability of a negative response ($Q_i$) is the measure of conditional variance. In algebraic terms,

$$I(\theta) = \sum_{i=1}^{n} I_i(\theta) = \sum_{i=1}^{n} \frac{P_i'(\theta)^2}{P_i(\theta)Q_i(\theta)}, \qquad (4.5)$$

where $I(\theta)$ denotes test information and $I_i(\theta)$ denotes item information, with both conditional on θ.

**Information for Polytomous Models**

Conceptualizing information in terms of polytomous IRT models involves somewhat more complex considerations than for the dichotomous case. Nevertheless, the basic principles are the same, and the foregoing description highlights the fact that there are different ways to represent information. Specifically, it can be represented in terms of derivatives with respect to relevant functions (Equation 4.4), in terms of conditional expectations (as described in the context of the RSM), or in terms of sums of component elements (Equation 4.5).

Information in the context of polytomous IRT models also can be represented in these three ways. The additional complexities come partly from the fact that item categories provide an extra, more detailed level to the set of component elements. Furthermore, the probability of responding in a category ($P_{i_g}$) is no longer described by a single function but itself is based on the relationship among constituent boundary functions. Thus, information can be represented in terms of $P_{i_g}$, or equivalently, in terms of $P_{i_g}^*$, where the boundary functions do not independently define ICRFs but do so in conjunction with each other. One consequence of these additional considerations is that components can no longer simply be summed to provide higher levels of information. Instead, aggregating components of information in the polytomous context often requires weighted sums rather than simple sums.

We start with item categories as the most basic level of aggregation. Samejima (1977, 1988, 1996, 1998) notes that item category information, denoted here as $I_{i_g}(\theta)$, can be defined as the negative of the second derivative of the log of an ICRF:

$$I_{i_g}(\theta) = -\frac{\partial^2}{\partial \theta^2} \log P_{i_g}(\theta), \tag{4.6}$$

which Samejima (1998) notes is equivalent to

$$I_{i_g}(\theta) = \left\{ \frac{P'_{i_g}(\theta)}{P_{i_g}(\theta)} \right\}^2 - \frac{P''_{i_g}(\theta)}{P_{i_g}(\theta)}. \tag{4.7}$$

Information is evaluated conditionally with respect to $\theta$ (information varies as a function of $\theta$). The quantity described here as category information has the usual interpretation for information, being the direct indicant of measurement precision provided by a given category (Baker, 1992).

Because an item's categories are not independent of one another, it is not possible to simply define item information as a sum of category information, even though this might seem logical at first glance. Instead, an intermediary term must be constructed that represents the share of information that each category provides to item information. Category share information is obtained as a weighted component of category information, where $I_{i_g}$ is weighted by the response probability for a category across $\theta$. Category share information is therefore designated

$$I_{i_g}(\theta) P_{i_g}(\theta). \tag{4.8}$$

Item information is then a simple sum of category share information across all the categories of an item.

$$I_i = \sum_{g=0}^{m} I_{i_g} P_{i_g}. \tag{4.9}$$

Samejima (1969) noted that, in conditional expectation terms, this is equivalent to describing item information as the expected value of category information. That is

$$I_i = E[I_{i_g}|\theta].$$ (4.10)

Furthermore, Samejima shows that category share information can also be obtained by subtracting the second derivative of an ICRF from the squared first derivative of that function divided by the probability value of that function at each point across θ. In mathematical terms,

$$I_{i_g} P_{i_g} = \frac{(P'_{i_g})^2}{P_{i_g}} - P''_{i_g}.$$ (4.11)

Note that Equation 4.11 results from multiplying Equation 4.7 by $P_{i_g}$ as required by the definition of category share information in Equation 4.8.

Given the status of ICRFs in the GRM as being comprised of differences between adjacent CBRFs, Equation 4.11 also can be represented in category boundary terms (Samejima, 1969). With the usual notation of $P^*_{i_g}$ to represent a CBRF, Equation 4.11 becomes

$$I_{i_g} P_{i_g} = \frac{(P^{*\prime}_{i_g} - P^{*\prime}_{i_{g+1}})^2}{(P^*_{i_g} - P^*_{i_{g+1}})} - (P^{*\prime\prime}_{i_g} - P^{*\prime\prime}_{i_{g+1}}).$$ (4.12)

Then, from Equation 4.9, we know that we can obtain item information by simply summing either Equation 4.11 or Equation 4.12 over the categories of an item. However, Samejima (1969) also showed that the sum of the second derivatives of the ICRFs for an item equal zero. Thus, the elements to the right of the subtraction symbol in Equations 4.11 and 4.12 equal zero when summed across the categories of an item. Item information, when presented in terms of these two equations, therefore can be simplified to

$$I_i = \sum_{g=0}^{m} \frac{(P'_{i_g})^2}{P_{i_g}},$$ (4.13)

and in CBRF terms,

$$I_i = \sum_{g=0}^{m} \frac{(P^{*\prime}_{i_g} - P^{*\prime}_{i_{g+1}})^2}{(P^*_{i_g} - P^*_{i_{g+1}})}.$$ (4.14)

70

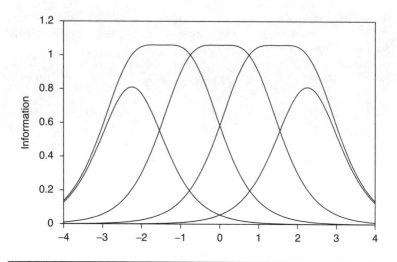

**Figure 4.1**     Category Information ($I_{i_g}$) for a Five-Category Item

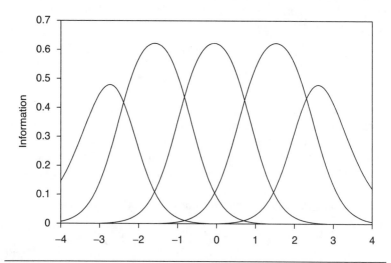

**Figure 4.2**     Category Share Information ($I_{i_g} P_{i_g}$) for a Five-Category Item

Figures 4.1 to 4.3 show examples of the category information, category share information, and item information, respectively, for the five-category item shown earlier in Figure 1.2. Note that this item is modeled with the more usual logistic version of the GRM. Interestingly, the category information

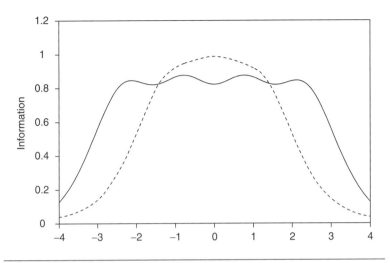

**Figure 4.3**     Item Information ($I_i$) for Two Five-Category Items

Note: Dashed lines are for an item with closer category boundaries.

functions for the normal ogive form of the GRM are dramatically different from those for the logistic GRM (see Samejima, 1983, for examples). However, subsequent information share and item information functions for the two manifestations of this model are very similar (Samejima, 1983). Figure 4.1 clearly shows that individual categories, in isolation, provide more information than do the same categories taken together (Figure 4.2).

Baker (1992), following Samejima (1975), notes that the distinction between response category information, $I_{i_g}$, and category share information, $I_{i_g} P_{i_g}$, exists only in polytomous IRT models. This provides a useful reminder of the differences between dichotomous and polytomous IRT models. A difference highlighted here is that polytomous item categories overlap in their contribution to item information (and therefore test information), hence the need for weighted rather than simple sums of category information in the aggregation process. This is another manifestation of the situation described earlier concerning the fact that category discrimination is complexly defined as a combination of the amount a category discriminates and the distance between category boundaries.

The issue of category width also arises in cases where widely spaced category boundaries produce multimodal information functions for the nonextreme categories. This occurred in the demonstration item in Figure 4.3. An example of an item information function for more closely spaced categories is shown with a dashed line in Figure 4.3. Here, the

72

category boundary locations are $b_{i_g}$= −1.25, −0.25, 0.25, and 1.25, for $g = 1, \ldots, 4$, respectively, with $a_i$ again equal to 1.8. This dashed function is unimodal and also illustrates the fact that closer boundaries provide more information over a smaller range of the trait scale than do more widely spaced boundaries.

It is useful to recall that the amount of information provided by a polytomous item increases as the number of categories for an item increases (Samejima, 1969), resulting in smaller standard errors for respondents' trait estimates as categories are added (Baker, 1992). Thus, an advantage that arises from accepting the added complexity of polytomous discrimination and information is that polytomous items provide greater amounts of information than do dichotomous items.

## Relationship to Other IRT Models

The GRM occupies an interesting place among polytomous IRT models. As a difference model in Thissen and Steinberg's (1986) terminology, it constitutes the primary distinct type of polytomous IRT model to the Rasch and other divide-by-total models. However, as a member of Samejima's (1972) framework, it is related to the other models in the framework. In terms of models for ordered categorical data, this makes the GRM related to all of the divide-by-total models through their membership in the heterogeneous class of models (see Table 4.1).

### The Heterogeneous Case

Two features distinguish the heterogeneous case from the homogeneous case in Samejima's (1972) framework. Unlike the homogeneous case, which requires ordered data, the heterogeneous class of models in Samejima's framework can accommodate nominal data. Bock's (1972) NRM represents this element of the heterogeneous class of models.

At the theoretical level, however, the fundamental difference between Samejima's two classes of models is in the shape of the cumulative boundary functions, $P_{i_g}^*$. Whereas for models in the homogeneous case, these functions are the same shape within a given item, this need not be the case in the heterogeneous class of models, where the functions may have different shapes within an item (Samejima, 1988, 1996, 1997b).

Consider again the role, in the homogeneous case, of the $P_{i_g}^*$ functions, which is to define cumulative category boundaries that are used to obtain the probability of responding in any given category. Given this role, it would be a problem to have boundary functions with different slopes. The problem is that such functions would cross at some point on the trait continuum, leading to negative values for the differences that are meant to represent category response probabilities $(P^*_{i_g})$. It makes no sense, however, to have probabilities less than zero.

This problem is avoided in the models that represent the heterogeneous class because the $P^*_{i_g}$ do not serve the practical role of defining category response probabilities in these models. In other words, the parameters describing the shape of the $P^*_{i_g}$ are not estimated in the heterogeneous case. The category probabilities represented by ICRFs are instead obtained by other means for models that are members of the heterogeneous class of models. This has already been described for the most prominent members of this class, the polytomous Rasch models, the GPCM, and their variants.

Indeed, it is generally the case that heterogeneous model ICRFs *must* be obtained through some means other than estimating the parameters of the $P^*_{i_g}$ for use in Equation 1.2. The reason is that having a model with $P^*_{i_g}$ that can vary in shape within an item typically means that the functions are not the shape of logistic ogives (Thissen & Steinberg, 1986). This makes the task of estimating, or even defining, the parameters for such functions quite difficult, because the functions do not all have a simple common form.

It is possible to obtain the $P^*_{i_g}$ functions for models in the heterogeneous case by virtue of their definition as cumulative probability functions. However, in this case, the $P^*_{i_g}$ are obtained from the ICRFs rather than being used to produce the ICRFs, as they are in the homogeneous case. In the heterogeneous case, the $P^*_{i_g}$ are simply obtained by summing the probabilities of responding in the category or categories for the cumulative category boundary of interest and higher.

Representations for $P^*_{i_g}$ therefore can be produced for the Rasch and NRM ICRFs shown earlier. Figure 4.4 shows $P^*_{i_g}$ obtained by accumulating PCM ICRFs, whereas Figure 4.5 shows the $P^*_{i_g}$ obtained by accumulating the appropriate NRM ICRFs from Figure 2.1. Note that these functions are subtly different in shape. For both sets of functions, as one moves up the $\theta$ scale, we see functions whose asymptotes approach zero more quickly and simultaneously approach 1.0 more slowly. In other words, considering each ordered function in turn, we find that at any given value of $\theta$, the associated probability value is always higher for earlier $P^*_{i_g}$ than for later functions. This ensures that the functions do not cross, that they differ in shape, and results in functions that are not logistic (or normal) ogives in shape. (Note that even though the functions have an ogive-like *s* shape, in mathematical terms, they do not meet the formal requirements for logistic, or normal, ogives.)

It may be obvious that these functions serve no practical, model-building purpose. Indeed, the only role they have is at the theoretical level, where they define the heterogeneous class of polytomous IRT models, enabling

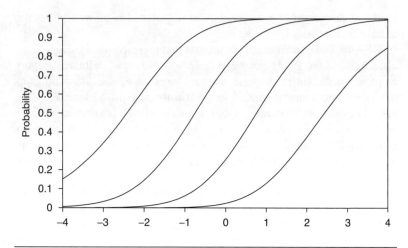

**Figure 4.4**     Heterogeneous Case $P_{i_g}^*$ Obtained by Accumulating PCM ICRFs

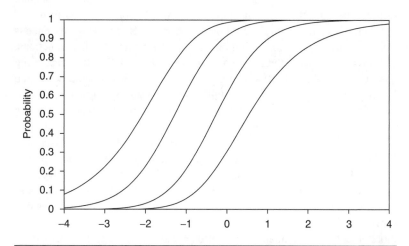

**Figure 4.5**     Heterogeneous Case $P_{i_g}^*$ Obtained by Accumulating NRM ICRFs

a level of comparison of the two distinct types of models within a common framework.

It is also of some interest that, even though Samejima (1972) was aware of the possibility of constructing models within the heterogeneous class in her theoretical framework, she concluded that they were unlikely to be useful or plausible (Samejima, 1979b, 1996, 1997a). As a result, she did not develop any specific, practical models within this theoretical class of models until quite recently, when she developed the acceleration model (Samejima, 1995). The acceleration model is an example of Samejima's ongoing interest in developing response models that represent a plausible psychological response process.

At a theoretical level, the acceleration model is itself, like the GRM, one of a family of potential acceleration-type models (Samejima, 1995, 1997b). As with the non-Samejima heterogeneous models, the acceleration model cannot be built on the cumulative category boundaries defined by $P_{i_g}^*$. Instead, in this case, it is constructed directly on the processing function $M_{i_g}^*$ (Samejima, 1995, 1997b), which was noted earlier to be the theoretical basis for the $P_{i_g}^*$.

The acceleration model was developed specifically to provide a way to model, in detail, complex cognitive tasks (Samejima, 1995). In this context, a test item becomes a cognitive task that is made up of a number of problem-solving steps that represent the item categories. The steps are modeled by parameters that are, in turn, modified by another parameter that represents a sum of the cognitive subprocesses that are required to complete each step of the task. In a sense, the acceleration model represents Samejima's exponential analog to the linear logistic models of Fischer described earlier.

## From Homogeneous Class to Heterogeneous Class and Back

It has been noted that it is possible to obtain cumulative category boundary functions, $P_{i_g}^*$, from item category functions, $P_{i_g}$, for all heterogeneous class models, whether or not the $P_{i_g}^*$ have an algebraic definition. This can be done even when the ICRFs have not been obtained from the $P_{i_g}^*$. This is despite the fact that the cumulative CBRFs ($P_{i_g}^*$) were originally introduced as the means of obtaining GRM ICRFs. The possibility of obtaining $P_{i_g}^*$ from $P_{i_g}$ is a trivial process for the GRM because the model is identified by having specific category probabilities ($P_{i_g}$) that result from differences between consecutive cumulative probabilities ($P_{i_g}^*$). Summing category probabilities to obtain cumulative probabilities is therefore hardly informative in the GRM case.

In contrast, summing category probabilities to obtain cumulative boundaries is the practical mechanism that makes concrete the existence of the heterogeneous class as a component of Samejima's (1972) framework. Were it not possible to obtain $P_{i_g}^*$ from $P_{i_g}$, it would not be possible to compare the NRM, Rasch models, and Tutz and Samejima's sequential models with the GRM in the context of a common framework.

76

Saying that cumulative probabilities can be obtained as the sum of specific category probabilities can be expressed algebraically (Thissen & Steinberg, 1986) as

$$P_{i_g}^* = \sum_{g=g}^{m} P_{i_g}.$$ (4.15)

This, in turn, is equal to the ratio

$$P_{i_g}^* = \frac{\sum_{g=g}^{m} e^{Z_{i_g}}}{\sum_{g=1}^{m} e^{Z_{i_g}}}.$$ (4.16)

The exponential term, $Z_{i_g}$, varies from model to model in reasonably obvious ways, but several of the more relevant options will be laid out here. In the case of the NRM,

$$z_{i_g} = a_{i_g} \theta + c_{i_g}.$$ (4.17)

In the case of the PCM,

$$z_{i_g} = \theta + b_{i_g}.$$ (4.18)

In the case of the RSM,

$$z_{i_g} = \phi_i (\theta + b_i) + \kappa_g.$$ (4.19)

In the case of the ELM, that is, the scoring function formulation of the PCM,

$$z_{i_g} = \phi_i (\theta + b_i) + \kappa_{i_g}.$$ (4.20)

In the case of the GPCM,

$$z_{i_g} = a_i \left( \phi_i (\theta + b_i) + \sum \tau_{i_g} \right).$$ (4.21)

When the appropriate expression for $Z_{i_g}$ from Equations 4.17 to 4.21 is placed in Equation 4.16 and summed over the relevant categories in the numerator and denominator, a cumulative boundary function, $P_{i_g}^*$, results. These are defined in the same way as GRM $P_{i_g}^*$ in that they provide the probability of responding in category $g$ or higher. If one wants to think of $P^*_{i_g}$ purely as CBRFs, then this process describes how one can obtain globally defined CBRFs (the $P^*_{i_g}$) from locally defined, Rasch-type CBRFs. However, because these models are all examples of the heterogeneous class, the resulting $P^*_{i_g}$ need not be the same shape within an item. In fact, as already mentioned and shown in Figures 4.4 and 4.5, they are unlikely to even be logistic functions (Thissen & Steinberg, 1986).

Hemker (1996) addresses this issue by noting that divide-by-total models do not have a simple parametric form for cumulative category boundaries ($P^*_{i_g}$). Reciprocally, the difference models do not have a simple parametric form for locally defined, adjacent category boundaries.

However, in all other current examples of heterogeneous models, such as the adjacent category models, model parameters for functions other than $P^*_{i_g}$ are used to estimate ICRF probabilities. The ICRFs are then themselves used to obtain the shape of the $P^*_{i_g}$ if this is desired, through the process described above. The alternative ICRF model parameters include locally defined category boundary locations, or item and threshold locations. Typically, these are obtained in the context of divide-by-total (usually Rasch model) format.

## A Common Misconception

We hope that the foregoing discussion of heterogeneous class models in Samejima's (1972) framework will have made reasonably clear what $P^*_{i_g}$ represents in the context of these models. Specifically, these cumulative functions are, in a sense, artificial constructions based on model parameters obtained in other contexts—often by first modeling items with a polytomous Rasch model. It is worthwhile, however, clarifying precisely what the $P^*_{i_g}$ do not represent in the heterogeneous case.

Samejima (1969) initially developed the GRM, and did so on the basis of 2PL-defined $P^*_{i_g}$ CBRFs, where the boundary discriminations can differ across items but not within items. This is the classic example of a specific model in the homogeneous case in her framework. Her subsequent expansion of the framework to include the heterogeneous case, where models are defined by $P^*_{i_g}$ that differ in shape *within* items, seems to have led occasionally to the impression that this means that "the" heterogeneous model is one where $P^*_{i_g}$ CBRFs are estimated using the 2PL model with item discriminations allowed to vary within items. This is not the case, and there is actually no such model. Estimating cumulative CBRFs in this way would result in crossing boundary functions, which would then produce negative category probabilities when $P^*_{i_g}$ differences were taken according to Equation 1.2.

Even the tactic of artificially constraining boundary differences to be positive does not solve the problem of crossing boundaries; it only avoids the problem of negative probabilities at the cost of having segments of the trait continuum where the sum of probabilities in all categories fails to add up to 1.0. This is a poor solution that tries to make the misrepresentation of heterogeneous case models into a workable model.

Ultimately, the only specific models in the heterogeneous class are models such as the NRM in the nominal case, together with the polytomous Rasch models and the acceleration model in the ordered categorical case. There is no such entity as a specific heterogeneous GRM.

## Variations

### Continuous Response Model

A variation of the GRM developed by Samejima (1973) is the continuous response model (CRM). This model is for data where responses can be made at any point on the response continuum, rather than being restricted to a finite set of discrete categories. The CRM can be thought of as a variation of the GRM because Samejima develops it as the limiting case of the ordered response situation. This is done in a manner similar to the approach described earlier for Müller's (1987) continuous Rasch model. Specifically, beginning with a finite segment of the response continuum, Samejima (1973) postulates an ordered categorical response situation with categories of equal size. These are successively halved in size until, in the extreme case of an infinite number of partitionings, the "categories" represent every point on the continuum, thereby degenerating to the continuous response level.

The CRM is also a variation of the GRM in that Samejima (1973) develops it within the homogeneous class of models in her framework. Müller's (1987) continuous Rasch model is an example of a continuous response model in Samejima's (1972) heterogeneous class of models.

The $P^*$ functions can be modeled any number of ways in the CRM. Samejima (1973) outlines three possibilities for a continuous response type of model, the normal ogive and logistic functions, as well as a hybrid, double exponential function. Parameter estimation is a problem, and a solution is found only for the normal ogive-based model. Because this is the only practical implementation of the potential models, it is the model referred to above as the CRM.

### Multiple-Choice GRM

Another interesting variant of the GRM is provided by Samejima (1979b). Previously, we introduced Samejima's modification of Bock's

(1972) NRM, which allows for the possibility of modeling respondent guessing. If the response options of multiple-choice items have a known (or previously identified) order with respect to the latent trait, then these items could be modeled by the GRM instead of the NRM, which is required only when responses are unordered. However, the concern with guessing in the face of multiple-choice items would then remain. Samejima (1979b) shows that her modification for the NRM can be equally well applied to the usual logistic function version of the GRM as well as the less common normal ogive version, if either of these models is being applied to multiple-choice data.

*Rating Scale GRM*

Muraki (1990) develops a variant of the GRM that is also applied to both the logistic and normal ogive versions of the model. Muraki's contribution is to constrain the GRM into a form that is targeted to rating scales, that is, he develops a rating scale GRM (RS-GRM). He does this by reparameterizing the GRM CBRF location parameter, $b_{i_g}$, into a single item location parameter, $b_i$, and a set of boundary location parameters, $c_g$, so that $P^*_{i_g}$ in the logistic version of the RS-GRM is now represented by

$$P^*_{i_g} = \frac{e^{a_i(\theta - b_i + c_g)}}{1 + e^{a_i(\theta - b_i + c_g)}}, \tag{4.24}$$

instead of Equation 4.1.

This reparameterization is formally equivalent to the way the RSM is reparameterized relative to the PCM (Equations 3.1 and 3.5, respectively). The rationale for the reparameterization is also the same, that is, that adopting a rating scale for a set of items implies that the scale should be operating equivalently across items. This implies that specific categories should be the same size across items and not unique to each item. This is accomplished, in the RS-GRM, by estimating a single set of category boundary parameters, $c_g$, that is applied to all items that differ only in their scale location, which is indexed by the parameter $b_i$.

It is important to realize, however, that the RS-GRM category boundary parameters, $c_g$, are not the same parameters as the RSM threshold parameters, $\tau_g$, although both serve the same function. The $c_g$ are obtained in the global item context of GRM item location parameters, whereas the $\tau_g$ are obtained in the adjacent category context of Rasch model item location parameters.

The RS-GRM also differs from the RSM in that it can include an item discrimination parameter as well as a location parameter. Thus, although the category boundary locations are expected to be the same across items using the same rating scale, the items are permitted to vary in discrimination. This makes the RS-GRM closer to a rating scale version of the GPCM (or a generalized RSM) than the RSM itself, in terms of item parameters that may vary. Muraki (1990) does, however, also demonstrate an RS-GRM application with discrimination fixed across items. This form of the model is more directly comparable to the RSM in terms of parametric complexity.

It is interesting to note that, although the justification for the RS-GRM is the same as for the RSM, Muraki's motivation for developing the RS-GRM is actually to be able to separate the estimation of item parameters from that of the category boundary parameters. The demonstrated reason for this is so that he could compare changes in item location over time by looking at a single item parameter while keeping category boundaries fixed.

**Summary of Samejima Models**

Samejima (1972) developed a comprehensive framework for extended item formats. The framework arguably encompasses all polytomous IRT models. She has developed three models within this framework: the GRM (two versions), the CRM, and the acceleration model. In addition to her specific models, Samejima also developed a modification for the NRM and the GRM to accommodate potential guessing in multiple-choice items. Much of her more recent work has also focused on nonparametric IRT estimation procedures and other ways of obtaining cumulative boundary functions with more flexible shapes than that provided by a simple 2PL ogive.

Numerous other models have been described in Samejima's work in theoretical terms or as practical possibilities without ever being developed to a usable level. The logistic version of the GRM has been the model most commonly used by other researchers. This IRT extension of Thurstone's method of successive intervals has come to symbolize the global dichotomization approach to polytomous IRT model building that uses cumulative category boundaries as its basis. As such, the GRM is the only distinctive polytomous IRT modeling approach to the divide-by-total approach (NRM, Rasch models, and their variants) that has been used in psychometric research. The sequential model approach of Tutz (1990) and Samejima (1995) is a third distinctive approach but has yet to generate a substantial research profile.

Making comparisons between the two major approaches is not straightforward. Unlike the dichotomous case, where the Rasch, 2PL, and 3PL models form a nested hierarchy of models, at least in mathematical terms, there is no such relationship among the two major approaches to polytomous IRT modeling. Therefore, comparing polytomous Rasch models and the GRM in terms of their respective number of parameters to be estimated can be unhelpful. For example, extending the PCM by allowing a variable item discrimination parameter produces the GPCM, not the GRM. These are two fundamentally different models, even though they are both "2-parameter" polytomous models.

An important consequence of the different definition of the boundary location parameters is that it allows Rasch models, and other models based on adjacent category comparisons, to decompose discrimination into an item and a category component. The cumulative boundary approach underlying the GRM allows only item discrimination to vary. This provides the Rasch models and their variants the capacity to represent the structure of a polytomous item in a more complex manner than is possible for the GRM. It suggests that these models may be more flexible than the GRM.

If polytomous Rasch and similar models are more flexible than the GRM, it would be because the adjacent category approach is inherently more flexible than the cumulative boundary approach. That is, modeling only adjacent categories is less restrictive in data modeling terms than modeling cumulative boundaries.

A comparison of structural flexibility is difficult because of the different definitions of the respective location parameters and their distinctive functions. However, Samejima's framework provides a basis of comparison, essentially by converting category probabilities (from ICRFs) based on adjacent category boundaries into cumulative boundaries. As was mentioned earlier, such transformed boundaries need not be the same shape (hence the definition of heterogeneous models). This leads Samejima (1997b) to conclude that heterogeneous models (such as the polytomous Rasch models) are likely to better fit data given the resulting greater variety of possible ICRF shapes.

Direct empirical comparisons are difficult to construct and therefore rare. Maydeu-Olivares et al. (1994) found that each type of model better fit data generated following their own structure. However, Dodd's (1984) dissertation, with data that were not generated to fit either model, suggested that the PCM could hold its own against the GRM in terms of information provided, despite being a simpler model. This conclusion was further supported by the fact that a restricted GRM, with constrained discrimination, performed considerably more poorly than either the PCM or the GRM, even though it was included in the project as a fairer comparison for the simpler PCM.

## Potential Weaknesses of the Cumulative Boundary Approach

In terms of sheer number of model variations, the adjacent category approach is clearly superior to the cumulative approach of the GRM. This flexibility was noted earlier as a strength of polytomous Rasch models. Kelderman's (1984) loglinear model framework is an example of this flexibility. Complementary work by Agresti (1997) describes general relationships between Rasch models and loglinear models for unordered and ordered categorical data. In this work, Agresti also describes relationships between these models and a cumulative boundaries model that is very closely related to Samejima's (1969) GRM. Despite this tenuous link to the more general statistical context of loglinear models, the cumulative boundaries approach underlying the GRM does not appear to embody the same level of flexibility as is found in polytomous Rasch models.

## Possible Strengths of the Cumulative Boundary Approach

The GRM does allow item discriminations to vary from item to item, but relaxing the specific objectivity requirements of Rasch models allows them to also be extended in this way, as in the case of the GPCM. However, if the choice is made to pursue flexibility in the area of discrimination, the adjacent category approach is still more flexible because it allows the possibility of varying not only item discrimination but also category-level discrimination. This cannot be done in the GRM because of the resulting negative probabilities. However, being able to model category-level discrimination enhances model flexibility by enabling models with the capacity to model partly ordered and partly nominal data (e.g., the OPM), null categories, and completely ordinal data (NRM).

The area in which the GRM has a less equivocal advantage over adjacent category models is with respect to the issue of the meaning of the boundary location parameter. The interpretation of the boundary location parameter is unambiguous in the case of cumulatively defined boundaries and sequential models. However, it is not clear how one should interpret this parameter in the case of locally defined, adjacent category boundaries. It is generally agreed that it cannot legitimately be interpreted as modeling sequential response steps, as was initially proposed. What is not clear, however, is whether the ambiguous interpretation of this parameter has any important measurement consequences, over and above the conceptual difficulties that it raises.

Samejima's research on polytomous item information has application across both major types of polytomous IRT models. Much of this application has been in the context of implementing polytomous item CAT procedures, although it is also useful for guiding test construction. The widespread applicability of her work on information complements Samejima's theoretical framework by providing a valuable practical tool that spans the spectrum of polytomous IRT models.

TABLE 4.2
Parameter Values and Response Probabilities
for a Morality Item Using the Graded Response Model

| Model | | *1* | *2* | *3* | *4* |
|---|---|---|---|---|---|
| | | | | *i* | |
| GRM | $a_i = 0.719$ | | | | |
| | $b_{i_g}$ | −3.558 | −0.878 | 1.146 | 4.114 |

| | | | Item Category | | |
|---|---|---|---|---|---|
| | *1* | *2* | *3* | *4* | *5* |
| $p\|\theta = -1.5$ | 0.185 | 0.425 | 0.260 | 0.112 | 0.017 |
| $p\|\theta = 1.5$ | 0.026 | 0.128 | 0.284 | 0.431 | 0.132 |

## A Practical Example

The same Likert-type response example item used to demonstrate the PCM, RSM, and GPCM is also used in the following practical example demonstrating the GRM. As was the case with the GPCM, five unique parameters must be estimated to model our example item with the GRM. The unique item discrimination parameter and four unique boundary location parameters are shown in Table 4.2. It must be remembered, however, that in this case, the $b_{i_g}$ represent the locations of cumulative boundary functions. Because these are a different type of function to the boundary functions of any other model for which practical examples have previously been provided, it is not meaningful to directly compare location parameters, even where the same item is being modeled.

An example of the differences between the two types of boundary location parameters is that GRM-modeled CBRF locations are always, invariably sequential, unlike adjacent category boundary locations. However, it is still possible to obtain diagnostic information about item category functioning from GRM ICRFs, which will represent potentially problematic categories as "never most probable" in the same way that adjacent category model ICRFs do. Note that when modeled by the GRM, there is a segment of the trait continuum where a response is most probable for each of the five categories of our example item. That is, as was the case when this item was modeled by the adjacent category models, there is no category that is never the most probable category at any point on the trait continuum. This is demonstrated graphically in the GRM ICRFs shown in Figure 4.6.

Although it is not meaningful to compare CBRFs across adjacent category and cumulative boundary models, the response probabilities modeled

84

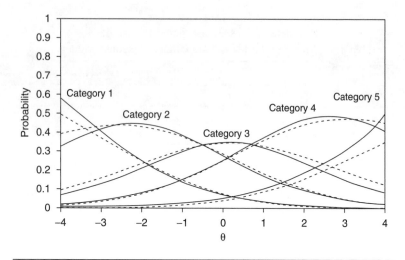

**Figure 4.6**    ICRFs for a Likert-Type Morality Item Modeled by the GRM

Key: Solid line = GRM; dashed line = GPCM.

by the ICRFs are the same type of probability across both types of models. Therefore, response probabilities can be compared at specific trait levels, such as those shown in Table 3.4. Equivalent response probabilities for each item category, as modeled by the GRM, at $\theta = -1.5$ and $\theta = 1.5$ are shown in the bottom half of Table 4.2. These probabilities show that Category 2 is the most probable response at $\theta = -1.5$, whereas at $\theta = 1.5$, the most probable response category is Category 4. This is the same result as was obtained for the PCM and the GPCM. Perusal of specific response probability values, at both trait levels and across all five categories, shows that the probabilities obtained for the GRM are very similar to the GPCM results (see Table 3.4). A more comprehensive demonstration of this similarity is provided in Figure 4.6, where GPCM ICRFs are superimposed as dashed lines over the solid GRM ICRFs.

   The similarity of the two sets of results is likely to be due to the fact that both the GRM and GPCM specifically model a discrimination parameter for each item, rather than constraining discrimination to a fixed value as occurs for the PCM and RSM. It is particularly interesting that, ultimately, each of the five categories' response probabilities for the two models is so similar despite the model's respective ICRFs being built on very different types of CBRFs and, effectively, very different types of discrimination parameters. In effect, what has happened is that distinctively different parameter values have been estimated for each model's different types of $a_i$ and $b_{i_g}$ parameters. This is most noticeable in the divergent $a_i$ values (GRM $a_i$ = 0.719; GPCM $a_i$ = 0.395). Yet when these divergent values for the distinctive types of discrimination and boundary location parameters are combined within both types of model, they result in very similar category response probabilities across the trait continuum for our example item.

## 5. MODEL SELECTION

The models described above were each introduced by their developers with a particular rationale in mind. Generally, little empirical evidence has been tendered to substantiate the rationales for each model, and, in the case of the PCM, the original rationale for its development had been demonstrated to be invalid (e.g., see Molenaar, 1983; Verhelst & Verstralen, 1997; and the earlier discussion of item "steps"). Nevertheless, each model has come to acquire a life of its own, often finding potential application in contexts beyond the reasons for their original development. For example, each of these eight models can legitimately be applied to modeling Likert-type rating data, even though only three of them were explicitly developed to do so (RSM, SIM, and RS-GRM). The question remains as to how a measurement practitioner should choose from among the range of models available.

### General Criteria

Data characteristics will often simplify a practitioner's choice. For example, if the data are scored dichotomously, then the choice between an adjacent category and a cumulative boundaries model becomes moot. Similarly, continuous or nominally scored data preclude the use of a model for ordered categorical data unless some data manipulation is performed first. Finally, if all items to be modeled do not have the same number of categories, then a rating scale model is ruled out.

Beyond data characteristics, models can be selected on the basis of measurement philosophy. Samejima (1995, 1996, 1997b) argues that the fundamental issue in measurement is whether or not a model faithfully reflects the psychological reality that produced the data, and she provides a set of specific mathematical criteria for testing a model. In contrast, Rasch model proponents argue that the related principles of specific objectivity and fundamental measurement, which some Rasch models (but no non-Rasch models) meet, should be the criteria by which models are chosen. Specific objectivity (Rasch, 1966) requires that comparisons among item parameters be independent of person parameter values, and vice versa. This is closely related to the mathematical principle underlying sufficient statistics (Rasch, 1977; van der Linden, 1994).

## Mathematical Approaches

Selecting IRT models based on mathematical criteria typically involves some method for assessing model-data fit, where the model that appears to best fit a set of data is selected. One such method is to graphically analyze fit. An exploratory heuristic (Kingston & Dorans, 1985) involves comparing model-predicted response functions with empirical response functions (McKinley & Mills, 1985, 1989). A more formal approach is to graphically analyze residuals (Ludlow, 1985, 1986), where residuals are essentially the difference between a person's observed and expected response.

### Statistical Fit Tests

The most common method for attempting to assess model-data fit is to use some form of statistical fit test. These can be grouped into four general classes: residual-based measures, multinomial distribution-based tests, response function-based tests, and Guttman error-based tests.

Fit measures can also be classified in terms of the level of generality of their application. Fit can be assessed at the global level in terms of the fit of an entire dataset from a complete measurement instrument. It can also be assessed in terms of the fit of specific groups of items from a test, if specific hypotheses about fit are to be tested. Finally, fit can be assessed in terms of the fit of individually modeled items to a set of data.

### Residual-Based Measures

For direct residual-based measures, a simple response residual comprises the difference between observed and expected item responses. This can be standardized by dividing the residual by the standard deviation of the observed score (Masters & Wright, 1997; Wright & Masters, 1982; Wu, 1997).

Response residuals can be summed over respondents to obtain an item fit measure. Generally, the accumulation is done with squared standardized residuals, which are then divided by the total number of respondents to obtain a mean square statistic. In this form, the statistic is referred to as an unweighted mean square (Masters & Wright, 1997; Wright & Masters, 1982) and has also come to be known as "outfit" (Smith, Schumacker, & Bush, 1998; Wu, 1997), perhaps because it is highly sensitive to outlier responses (Adams & Khoo, 1996; Smith et al., 1998; Wright & Masters, 1982).

A weighted version of this statistic was developed to counteract its sensitivity to outliers (Smith, 2000). In its weighted form, the squared standardized residual is multiplied by the observed response variance and then divided by the sum of the item response variances. This is sometimes referred to as an information weighted mean square and has become known as "infit" (Smith et al., 1998; Wu, 1997). Because the statistic is approximately distributed as a mean square, it is not symmetrical about the mean (Smith, 2000). Partly in an effort to obtain a statistic that allowed a single critical value (Smith et al., 1998), a cube root transformation of the mean square statistics was proposed. The resulting standardized statistics are referred to as unweighted and weighted $t$-statistics, respectively. They have approximate unit normal distributions.

*Multinomial Distribution-Based Tests*

In the context of general statistical theory, polytomous IRT models can be considered exponential models based on discrete data (Kelderman, 1996). Asymptotic goodness-of-fit statistics can be used with such data (Kelderman & Rijkes, 1994), with the most direct test of fit based on the multinomial distribution of response patterns, given that the model holds true (Andersen, 1997).

For $n$ items, each with $m$ categories, there are $n^m$ possible response patterns. The joint distribution of all response patterns has the same likelihood as the multinomial distribution (Andersen, 1997). A fitted model can be tested against the general multinomial model by comparing observed and expected frequencies for the response patterns. A number of test statistics that are asymptotically distributed as $\chi^2$ are available to test differences between observed and expected frequencies (Kelderman, 1996). These include Pearson's $\chi^2$, the log-likelihood ratio statistic ($\chi^2$), the Freeman-Tukey statistic, and the Neyman modified $\chi^2$. These are themselves all special cases of a general statistic for the fit of observed to expected frequencies (Cressie & Read, 1984). Cressie and Read also provided a compromise statistic for use when the type of alternative hypothesis being tested is unknown, as is usually the case in model testing. This class of fit tests is particularly relevant in the context of MLE (Baker, 1992), which is prevalent in IRT model estimation.

*Response Function-Based Tests*

This type of fit assessment was initially proposed as a means for studying person fit. In this approach, instead of observed and expected frequencies of response patterns, observed and expected log-likelihoods of individual item responses are subtracted and standardized (Rost & von Davier, 1994).

*Guttman Error-Based Tests*

An alternative to the response function-based tests is to take a nonparametric approach consisting of counting the number of Guttman response errors across item pairs. A more comprehensive approach is to weight the Guttman errors. The $Q_i$ statistic (Rost & von Davier, 1994) is such a statistic and is essentially a ratio of log-likelihood ratios (Karabatsos, 2000). The test is a simple function of conditional item response patterns, Guttman response patterns, and anti-Guttman response patterns.

## Fit Statistic Problems

Each of the four general approaches to statistically testing fit has its own problems. The residual measures are based on unknown distributional properties (Masters & Wright, 1997), which some consider to be dubious (Rogers & Hattie, 1987). The lack of known distributional properties makes it difficult to justify critical values for the test statistic, with the result that several different values have been proposed (Ludlow & Haley, 1992; Smith et al., 1998; Wu, 1997).

The major difficulty with any of the multinomial distribution-based $\chi 2$ tests is that they require impossibly large response samples when more than a dozen items with three or four response categories each are used. Otherwise, the expected frequencies of response patterns become small and the test statistics' approximations to a $\chi^2$ distribution become poor (Kelderman, 1996).

Although the response function-based approach is promising, very little research has been conducted using it in the context of polytomous IRT models. Concerns remain regarding the asymptotic properties of the statistics, particularly with estimated model parameters and in the face of model violations. Similarly, the main drawback of the $Q_i$ statistic is that there has been very little research to determine whether it operates as intended.

Two general problems arise with tests of model fit. First, the power of all the fit tests described above depends strongly on the variance of the statistic (Rost & von Davier, 1994). That is, when item trait locations are close to respondents' $\theta$ levels, there is no good way to know whether there is lack of fit. This is a well-recognized problem with no obvious solution. Furthermore, as with all inferential test statistics, these fit tests are sensitive to sample size. Given sufficiently large sample sizes, even small deviations from model fit will be identified as statistically significant.

An important theoretical concern also threatens the validity of fit tests. Baker (1992) notes that, in practice, IRT modeling involves the application of curve-fitting techniques to the observed proportions of category responses in the hope that fit is sufficiently adequate to justify faith in the model being fitted. However, Garcia-Pérez and Frary (1991) point out that testing fit under this approach involves the fundamental contradiction that fit is measured after parameters are estimated in order to fit the model as well as possible. In other words, it is not possible to test the fit of IRT models against data because there is no way to test the adequacy of modeled response functions independently of the parameter estimation process (Garcia-Pérez & Frary, 1991).

A more sophisticated approach to choosing a model than solely considering fit statistics is to simultaneously take into account the goodness of fit of a model and the number of parameters modeled to achieve that fit (Sclove, 1987). This typically involves a penalty term that increases with the number of parameters in the fitted models. Akaike's information criterion (AIC) (Akaike, 1977) implements a form of model selection along these lines and has occasionally been used in IRT (e.g., Wilson, 1992; Wilson & Adams, 1993, 1995). Some research suggests that the AIC is not asymptotically consistent (see Sclove, 1987), and it is not clear that the AIC is appropriate for comparing models with different types of parameters, such as adjacent category and cumulative boundary models.

An extension of the AIC that is based on the likelihood ratio of two comparison models rather than a single baseline model (Maydeu-Olivares et al., 1994) is the ideal observer index (IOI) (Levine, Drasgow, Williams, McCusker, & Thomasson, 1992). This index is more appropriate than the AIC when comparing models with different types of parameters. However, the asymptotic statistical properties of this index have not been well investigated, and there is some indication that it is sensitive to both test length and sample size (Maydeu-Olivares et al., 1994). Furthermore, computation of the IOI is not straightforward, in part because the index is estimated in a simulation study that involves a high burden of time and effort (van Engelenburg, 1997). Ultimately, this index is more suitable as a research tool than a practical method for choosing among models in a practical testing context.

## An Example

A simple demonstration of the use of fit tests with the data used in the PCM, RSM, GPCM, and GRM practical examples from the previous two chapters is provided here. The estimated item parameter values for the four models are provided again in Table 5.1. This helps to remind us that the RSM is the most restrictive model of the four, whereas the GPCM and GRM are the least restrictive models by virtue of the number and type of parameters estimated. Table 5.1 also provides $p$ values for individual item fit statistics for the item that was modeled to provide these parameter values.

TABLE 5.1

Parameter Values and Fit Statistic $p$ Values for a Morality
Item Using the Partial Credit Model, the Rating Scale Model, the
Generalized Partial Credit Model, and the Graded Response Model

| | | | $i$ | | | Fit Tests | |
| Model | | 1 | 2 | 3 | 4 | $\chi^2$ | $Q_i$ |
|---|---|---|---|---|---|---|---|
| PCM | $b_{i_g}$ | −1.618 | − 0.291 | 0.414 | 2.044 | 0.000 | 0.102 |
| RSM | $b_{i_g} = b_i + \tau_g$ | −1.233 | − 0.455 | 0.471 | 1.837 | 0.000 | 0.027 |
| GPCM | $a_i = 0.395$ | | | | | | |
| | $b_{i_g}$ | −3.419 | − 0.482 | 0.777 | 4.240 | 0.143 | |
| GRM | $a_i = 0.719$ | | | | | | |
| | $b_{i_g}$ | −3.558 | − 0.878 | 1.146 | 4.114 | 0.009 | |

PARSCALE (Muraki & Bock, 1999) provides a multinomial distribution-based $\chi^2$ test of item fit for each model. The $p$ values in Table 5.1 show that this item best fits the GPCM, fits the GRM somewhat less well, and fits the PCM and RSM least well, with no differentiation among the last two models in terms of probability of fit. By comparison, WinMira (von Davier, 2000) provides a Guttman error-based standardized $Q_i$ statistic, but only for the PCM and RSM. This program does not estimate GPCM or GRM parameters. Unlike the PARSCALE fit test, the $Q_i$ statistic is able to distinguish between the PCM and RSM, in probability terms, showing that the more restrictive RSM has a distinctly poorer probability of fitting this item.

Tests of fit were also provided by each program for the entire 12-item questionnaire from which this example item was taken. However, even with almost 1,000 responses to the 12 items, these data were still too sparse to reliably estimate the overall fit statistics.

### Differences in Modeled Outcome

Underlying most methods for choosing among different IRT models is the implicit assumption that the models produce different results. However, there is little demonstrated evidence that different polytomous IRT models do produce substantially different measurement outcomes when applied to the same data. Some of the few comparative studies of polytomous IRT models suggest that it is of little consequence which model is used (e.g., Dodd, 1984; Maydeu-Olivares et al., 1994; Ostini, 2001; van Engelenburg, 1997; Verhelst et al., 1997).

In the context of a discussion about the consequences of choosing the "wrong" model, Wainer and Thissen (1987) note that inaccuracies in the estimation of item parameters becomes error in the θ estimates. However, in their research with dichotomous models, they found that the bias in trait estimation that resulted from using the wrong response model was small and could be corrected, to some extent, by using robust estimation techniques. On the other hand, Yen (1981) listed potential problems with fitting the wrong dichotomous model to a given data set. Similar research does not yet exist for polytomous IRT models.

Unfortunately, common software routines for implementing different polytomous models typically employ different fit tests, which can produce widely different indications of model fit (Ostini, 2001). The result is that reliance on model/software specific fit indicators can result in different data being excluded from analyses, which subsequently results in the appearance of differences in model functioning, even though the difference is primarily the effect of fit test variations.

## Conclusion

Considering the fundamental structural differences between the two major types of polytomous IRT models, it is certainly a matter of some interest as to whether they produce demonstrable, meaningful differences in measurement outcome. It is not clear that this question can be answered by recourse to statistical procedures, either graphical or goodness-of-fit tests. A definitive conclusion also will not always be provided by considerations of the different measurement philosophies implicit in the two approaches. In part, this is because the importance of specific objectivity is not universally agreed upon. However, it is also partly due to the fact that there are models based on adjacent categories that do not meet the requirements for models to provide specific objectivity. Therefore, in the case of polytomous models, differences in measurement philosophy do not boil down to the question of specific objectivity. Similarly, Samejima's criteria do not automatically rule out adjacent category models. So, even philosophical criteria may not differentiate polytomous IRT models.

Ultimately, the best approach to model selection should begin with a consideration of data characteristics. It may then be influenced by measurement philosophy considerations. Tests of model data would then ideally involve input from multiple sources, including tests of specific model assumptions, as well as goodness-of-fit tests, either graphical or statistical, or both, together with sound judgment and substantive expertise.

## ACRONYMS AND GLOSSARY

$\theta$ **parameter** person parameter, indicates person's standing on latent trait
*a* **parameter** item discrimination parameter

**adjacent boundary measurement approach** basis of Rasch-type polytomous IRT models, where category boundaries are calculated solely on
the basis of category probabilities for adjacent pairs of categories (contrast with **cumulative boundary measurement approach**)

*b* **parameter** item location parameter, also called item difficulty parameter
in ability testing

**BLM** binomial logistic model; the simplest constrained, polytomous version
of the rating scale model

**categorical data** from a variable whose values can only take the form of
(usually a small set of) integers (e.g., Likert-type data); that is, there are gaps
between possible values that the variable can take; also called discrete data

**CBRF** category boundary response function. Also called
category characteristic curve (CCC);
category response function (CRF);
cumulative category response function;
item characteristic curve (ICC)

**CCC** category characteristic curve, see CBRF and ICRF

**continuous data** from a variable whose values can (at least theoretically)
take the form of any real number (e.g., temperature); that is, there are
an infinite number of possible values (with no gaps between) that the
variable can take

**CRF** category response function, see CBRF and ICRF

**CRM** continuous response model; a generalization of the GRM

**CTT** classical test theory, also called true score and error theory, or just true
score theory

**cumulative boundary measurement approach** basis of Thurstone/
Samejima-type polytomous IRT models, where category boundaries are
calculated on the basis of cumulative category probabilities (contrast
with **adjacent boundary measurement approach**)

**dichotomous** two-category item response format; for example, items with
*true/false, yes/no,* or *right/wrong* as response options

**DLM** dispersion, location model; a constrained version of the rating scale
model

**DSLM** dispersion, skew, location model; a constrained version of the
rating scale model

**ELM** extended logistic model; a generic label for the scoring function
formulation of the partial credit model

**GPCM** generalized partial credit model; a polytomous item response
theory model

**graded responses** ordered responses. Responses collected from an item
with explicitly ordered response categories; for example, a five-category
item with categories ranging from *strongly disagree* to *strongly agree*

**GRM** graded response model; a polytomous item response theory model

**ICIF** item category information function

**ICRF** item category response function. Also called
category characteristic curve (CCC);
category probability curve;
category response function (CRF);
item-option characteristic curve;
model probability curve;
operating characteristic (OC);
operating characteristic curve (OCC);
operating characteristic function (OCF);
operating response function (ORF);
option response function;
response probability curve

**IIF** item information function

**information** a statistically defined indicator of measurement quality. Closely
related to the discriminating power of an item and inversely related to measurement error. Varies as a function of $\theta$

**IRIF** item response information function (Samejima, 1983); or, the information function for individual categories in a polytomous item (Parscale)

**IRF** item response function; defined, in polytomous models, as the conditional mean of item scores given $\theta$

**IRT** item response theory, also called latent trait theory

**latent class analysis** analysis arising from the application of a latent class
model

**latent class model** like IRT, a latent trait model, but one where the latent
trait is assumed to take on a finite set of values, called classes

**latent trait** unobservable psychological construct hypothesized or assumed
to underlie item responses

**linear integer scoring function** a simplified scoring function that results
from fixing threshold discrimination at 1.0. Scoring function values then
simply become the number of boundaries traversed, which is the same as
the category score when $m + 1$ categories are scored $0, 1, \ldots, m$ (see also
**scoring function**)

**local independence** items are statistically independent (not correlated)
for all respondents at a given trait level. Conversely, this means that the
relationships-among items in a test are due entirely to the latent trait
being measured

**monotonic** characteristic of a function that refers to the fact that it never
changes direction. For example, increasing ogival functions never decrease
at any point along the function

**normal ogive** S-shaped curve that plots the proportion of the area under the
normal curve as a function of $z$ score. Originally used to represent the
shape of IRT IRFs

**OCC** operating characteristic curve, see ICRF

**ordered responses** another term for graded responses

**OPM** ordered partition model; a polytomous item response theory model

**ORF** operating response function, see ICRF

**PCM** partial credit model; a polytomous item response theory model

**polytomous** item response format with more than two categories, that is, multiple response options; for example, *strongly disagree* to *strongly agree* (Likert-type), and multiple-choice formats, or test questions that allow part marks

**processing function** represents the response process underlying models in Samejima's general framework. Specifically, a function describing the probability of being attracted to a particular category $g$, over and above an attraction to the previous category, $g - 1$

**RS-DLM** rating scale version of the dispersion, location model

**RS-GRM** rating scale version of the GRM

**RSM** rating scale model; a polytomous item response theory model

**scoring function** a sum of category threshold discriminations up to the category being modeled (see also **linear integer scoring function**)

**SIM** successive intervals model; a polytomous Rasch model incorporating elements of the rating scale model and the dispersion location model

**SLM** simple logistic model; generic term for the dichotomous Rasch model or 1PL model

**thresholds** a type of category boundary; where boundaries are defined with respect to a single item trait location; term often used in Rasch rating scale research

**TIF** test information function

**TRF** test response function, or test characteristic curve; summated IRFs from all items in a (usually dichotomous) test

# NOTES

1. Mathematical treatments of ordered polytomous models conventionally (for algebraic convenience, though not for ease of exposition) number categories from 0 to $m - 1$ (0 to 4 in our five-category example). This results in the form of Equation 1.2 used above where the first category is set to zero ($g = 0$ in Figure 1.4). The alternative to this is the intuitive approach of labeling the first category as 1 (the number inside the circle in Figure 1.4). Taking this approach requires the right-hand side of Equation 1.2 to be modified to read $P^*_{g-1} - P^*_g$. This form of the equation occasionally surfaces in the literature (e.g., Muraki & Carlson, 1995). Although the latter labeling approach is intuitively appealing, the former approach is

adopted here because (a) it is consistent with the way dichotomous IRT models are labeled, and (b) it is also consistent with the way categories are labeled in Rasch polytomous models. As will be shown, Rasch models use the expression $e^0$ to refer to the probability of responding in the first category. Using the latter labeling approach results in a more consistent notation where $e^0$ represents $P_0$ rather than $P_1$.

2. The ELM label is attractive because it highlights the place of the partial credit model as a general model that extends the dichotomous Rasch model, which can itself then be referred to as the simple logistic model (SLM) (Andrich, 1988b). The ELM nomenclature also avoids the unnecessary association of a general model with a particular application—that is, partial credit scoring.

## REFERENCES

ADAMS, R. (1988). Applying the partial credit model to educational analysis. *Applied Measurement in Education, 1,* 347–361.

ADAMS, R. J., & KHOO, S.-T. (1996). *Quest: The interactivce test analysis system, Version 2.1 for PowerPC Macintosh.* Melbourne: The Australian Council for Educational Measurement.

ADAMS, R. J., & WILSON, M. (1996). Formulating the Rasch model as a mixed coefficients multinomial logit. In G. Engelhard & M. Wilson (Eds.), *Objective measurement: Theory into practice* (Vol. 3, pp. 143–166). Norwood, NJ: Ablex.

AGRESTI, A. (1997). Connections between loglinear models and generalized Rasch models for ordinal responses. In J. Rost & R. Langeheine (Eds.), *Applications of latent trait and latent class models in the social sciences* (pp. 209–218). Münster: Waxmann.

AITCHISON, J., & BENNETT, J. A. (1970). Polychotomous quantal response by maximum indicant. *Biometrika, 57,* 253–262.

AITCHISON, J., & SILVEY, S. D. (1957). The generalization of probit analysis to the case of multiple responses. *Biometrika, 44,* 131–140.

AKAIKE, H. (1977). On entropy maximization principle. In P. R. Krishnaiah (Ed.), *Applications of statistics* (pp. 27–41). Amsterdam: North Holland.

ANDERSEN, E. B. (1973). Conditional inference for multiple-choice questionnaires. *British Journal of Mathematical and Statistical Psychology, 26,* 31–44.

ANDERSEN, E. B. (1977). Sufficient statistics and latent trait models. *Psychometrika, 42,* 69–81.

ANDERSEN, E. B. (1983). A general latent structure model for contingency table data. In H. Wainer & S. Messick (Eds.), *Principles of modern psychological measurement* (pp. 117–138). Hillsdale, NJ: Lawrence Erlbaum.

ANDERSEN, E. B. (1995). Polytomous Rasch models and their estimation. In G. H. Fischer & I. W. Molenaar (Eds.), *Rasch models: Foundations, recent developments, and applications* (pp. 271–291). New York: Springer-Verlag.

ANDERSEN, E. B. (1997). The rating scale model. In W. J. van der Linden & R. K. Hambleton (Eds.), *Handbook of modern item response theory* (pp. 67–84). New York: Springer.

ANDRICH, D. (1978a). Application of a psychometric rating model to ordered categories which are scored with successive integers. *Applied Psychological Measurement, 2,* 581–594.

96

ANDRICH, D. (1978b). A rating formulation for ordered response categories. *Psychometrika, 43,* 561–573.

ANDRICH, D. (1979). A model for contingency tables having an ordered response classification. *Biometrics, 35,* 403–415.

ANDRICH, D. (1982). An extension of the Rasch model for ratings providing both location and dispersion parameters. *Psychometrika, 47,* 105–113.

ANDRICH, D. (1985a). An elaboration of Guttman scaling with Rasch models for measurement. In N. B. Tuma (Ed.), *Sociological methodology* (pp. 33–80). San Francisco: Jossey-Bass.

ANDRICH, D. (1985b). A latent-trait model for items with response dependencies: Implications for test construction and analysis. In S. E. Embretson (Ed.), *Test design: Developments in psychology and psychometrics* (pp. 245–275). Orlando, FL: Academic Press.

ANDRICH, D. (1988a). A general form of Rasch's extended logistic model for partial credit scoring. *Applied Measurement in Education, 1,* 363–378.

ANDRICH, D. (1988b). *Rasch models for measurement.* Newbury Park, CA: Sage.

ANDRICH, D. (1995). Distinctive and incompatible properties of two common classes of IRT models for graded responses. *Applied Psychological Measurement, 19,* 101–119.

ANDRICH, D. (1996). Theoretical and empirical evidence on the dichotomization of graded responses. In G. Engelhard & M. Wilson (Eds.), *Objective measurement: Theory into practice* (Vol. 3, pp. 265–287). Norwood, NJ: Ablex.

BAKER, F. B. (1981). Log-linear, logit-linear models: A didactic. *Journal of Educational Statistics, 6,* 75–102.

BAKER, F. B. (1992). *Item response theory: Parameter estimation techniques.* New York: Marcel Dekker.

BARTHOLOMEW, D. J. (1987). *Latent variable and factor analysis.* London: Charles Griffin.

BEJAR, I. I. (1977). An application of the continuous response level model to personality measurement. *Applied Psychological Measurement, 1,* 509–521.

BIRNBAUM, A. (1968). Some latent trait models and their use in inferring an examinee's ability. In F. M. Lord & M. R. Novick (Eds.), *Statistical theories of mental test scores.* Reading, MA: Addison-Wesley.

BOCK, R. D. (1972). Estimating item parameters and latent ability when responses are scored in two or more nominal categories. *Psychometrika, 37,* 29–51.

BOCK, R. D. (1997a). A brief history of item response theory. *Educational Measurement: Issues and Practice, 16*(4), 21–33.

BOCK, R. D. (1997b). The nominal categories model. In W. J. van der Linden & R. K. Hambleton (Eds.), *Handbook of modern item response theory* (pp. 33–49). New York: Springer.

BRENNAN, R. L. (1998). Misconceptions at the intersection of measurement theory and practice. *Educational Measurement: Issues and Practice, 17*(1), 5–9, 13.

BURROS, R. H. (1955). The estimation of the discriminal dispersion in the method of successive intervals. *Psychometrika, 20,* 299–305.

CATTELL, J. M. (1890). Mental tests and measurements. *Mind, 15,* 373–380.

CHANG, H-H., & MAZZEO, J. (1994). The unique correspondence of the item response function and item category response functions in polytomously scored item response models. *Psychometrika, 59,* 391–404.

COHEN, J. (1983). The cost of dichotomization. *Applied Psychological Measurement, 7,* 249–253.

COOKE, D. J., & MICHIE, C. (1997). An item response theory analysis of the Hare Psychopathy Checklist–Revised. *Psychological Assessment, 9,* 3–14.

COX, E. P. (1980). The optimal number of response alternatives for a scale: A review. *Journal of Marketing Research, 17,* 407–422.

97

CRESSIE, N., & READ, T. R. C. (1984). Multinomial goodness-of-fit tests. *Journal of the Royal Statistical Society, Series B, 46,* 440–464.

DE AYALA, R. J. (1993). An introduction to polytomous item response theory models. *Measurement and Evaluation in Counseling and Development, 25,* 172–189.

DILLON, W. R., & GOLDSTEIN, M. (1984). *Multivariate analysis: Methods and applications.* New York: Wiley.

DODD, B. G. (1984). *Attitude scaling: A comparison of the graded response and partial credit latent trait models.* Unpublished doctoral dissertation, University of Texas, Austin.

DODD, B. G., & KOCH, W. R. (1994). Item and scale information functions for the successive intervals Rasch model. *Educational and Psychological Measurement, 54,* 873–885.

DRASGOW, F., LEVINE, M. V., TSIEN, S., WILLIAM, B., & MEAD, A. D. (1995). Fitting polytomous item response theory models to multiple-choice tests. *Applied Psychological Measurement, 19,* 143–165.

EDWARDS, A. L., & THURSTONE, L. L. (1952). An internal consistency check for scale values determined by the method of successive intervals. *Psychometrika, 17,* 169–180.

FISCHER, G. H., & PARZER, P. (1991). LRSM: Parameter estimation for the linear rating scale model. *Applied Psychological Measurement, 15,* 138.

FISCHER, G. H., & PONOCNY, I. (1994). An extension of the partial credit model with an application to the measurement of change. *Psychometrika, 59,* 177–192.

FISCHER, G. H., & PONOCNY, I. (1995). Extended rating scale and partial credit models for assessing change. In G. H. Fischer & I. W. Molenaar (Eds.), *Rasch models: Foundations, recent developments, and applications* (pp. 353–370). New York: Springer-Verlag.

FLANNERY, W. P., REISE, S. P., & WIDAMAN, K. F. (1995). An item response theory analysis of the general and academic scales of the Self-Description Questionnaire II. *Journal of Research in Personality, 29,* 168–188.

FRALEY, R. C., WALLER, N. G., & BRENNAN, K. A. (2000). An item response theory analysis of self-report measures of adult attachment. *Journal of Personality and Social Psychology, 78,* 350–365.

GARCIA-PÉREZ, M. A., & FRARY, R. B. (1991). Finite state polynomic item characteristic curves. *British Journal of Mathematical and Statistical Psychology, 44,* 45–73.

GLAS, C. A. W., & VERHELST, N. D. (1989). Extensions of the partial credit model. *Psychometrika, 54,* 635–659.

HAMBLETON, R. K., & SWAMINATHAN, H. (1985). *Item response theory: Principles and applications.* Boston: Kluwer Nijhoff.

HEMKER, B. T. (1996). *Unidimensional IRT models for polytomous items, with results for Mokken scale analysis.* Unpublished doctoral dissertation, University of Utrecht, The Netherlands.

HULIN, C. L., DRASGOW, F., & PARSONS, C. K. (1983). *Item response theory: Application to psychological measurement.* Homewood, IL: Dow Jones-Irwin.

JANSEN, P. G. W., & ROSKAM, E. E. (1986). Latent trait models and dichotomization of graded responses. *Psychometrika, 51,* 69–91.

KAMAKURA, W. A., & BALASUBRAMANIAN, S. K. (1989). Tailored interviewing: An application of item response theory for personality measurement. *Journal of Personality Assessment, 53,* 502–519.

KARABATSOS, G. (2000). A critique of Rasch residual fit statistics. *Journal of Applied Measurement, 1,* 152–176.

KELDERMAN, H. (1984). Loglinear Rasch model tests. *Psychometrika, 49,* 223–245.

KELDERMAN, H. (1996). Multidimensional Rasch models for partial-credit scoring. *Applied Psychological Measurement, 20,* 155–168.

98

KELDERMAN, H., & RIJKES, C. P. M. (1994). Loglinear multidimensional IRT models for polytomously scored items. *Psychometrika, 59,* 149–176.

KINGSTON, N. M., & DORANS, N. J. (1985). The analysis of item-ability regressions: An exploratory IRT model fit tool. *Applied Psychological Measurement, 9,* 281–288.

LAWLEY, D. N. (1943). On problems connected with item selection and test construction. *Proceedings of the Royal Society of Edinburgh, Series A, 23,* 273–287.

LEVINE, M. V., DRASGOW, F., WILLIAMS, B., McCUSKER, C., & THOMASSON, G. L. (1992). Measuring the difference between two models. *Applied Psychological Measurement, 16,* 261–278.

LIKERT, R. (1932). *A technique for the measurement of attitudes.* New York: R. S. Woodworth.

LORD, F. (1952). A theory of test scores. *Psychometric Monograph* (No. 7).

LORD, F. M. (1980). *Applications of item response theory to practical testing problems.* Hillsdale, NJ: Lawrence Erlbaum.

LORD, F. M., & NOVICK, M. R. (1968). *Statistical theories of mental test scores.* Reading, MA: Addison-Wesley.

LUDLOW, L. H. (1985). A strategy for the graphical representation of Rasch model residuals. *Educational and Psychological Measurement, 45,* 851–859.

LUDLOW, L. H. (1986). Graphical analysis of item response theory residuals. *Applied Psychological Measurement, 10,* 217–229.

LUDLOW, L. H., & HALEY, S. M. (1992). Polytomous Rasch models for behavioral assessment: The Tufts assessment of motor performance. In M. Wilson (Ed.), *Objective measurement: Theory into practice* (pp. 121–137). Norwood, NJ: Ablex.

MASTERS, G. N. (1982). A Rasch model for partial credit scoring. *Psychometrika, 47,* 149–174.

MASTERS, G. N. (1988a). The analysis of partial credit scoring. *Applied Measurement in Education, 1,* 279–297.

MASTERS, G. N. (1988b). Item discrimination: When more is worse. *Journal of Educational Measurement, 25,* 15–29.

MASTERS, G. N. (1988c). Measurement models for ordered response categories. In R. Langeheine & J. Rost (Eds.), *Latent traits and latent class models* (pp. 11–29). New York: Plenum.

MASTERS, G. N., & EVANS, J. (1986). Banking non-dichotomously scored items. *Applied Psychological Measurement, 10,* 355–367.

MASTERS, G. N., & WRIGHT, B. D. (1984). The essential process in a family of measurement models. *Psychometrika, 49,* 529–544.

MASTERS, G. N., & WRIGHT, B. D. (1997). The partial credit model. In W. J. van der Linden & R. K. Hambleton (Eds.), *Handbook of modern item response theory* (pp. 101–121). New York: Springer.

MAYDEU-OLIVARES, A., DRASGOW, F., & MEAD, A. D. (1994). Distinguishing among parametric item response models for polychotomous ordered data. *Applied Psychological Measurement, 18,* 245–256.

McKINLEY, R. L., & MILLS, C. N. (1985). A comparison of several goodness-of-fit statistics. *Applied Psychological Measurement, 9,* 49–57.

McKINLEY, R. L., & MILLS, C. N. (1989). Item response theory: Advances in achievement and attitude measurement. In B. Thompson (Ed.), *Advances in social science methodology* (pp. 71–135). Greenwich, CT: JAI.

MELLENBERGH, G. J. (1995). Conceptual notes on models for discrete polytomous item responses. *Applied Psychological Measurement, 19,* 91–100.

MISLEVY, R. J. (1996). Test theory reconceived. *Journal of Educational Measurement, 33,* 379–416.

MOLENAAR, I. W. (1983). *Item steps* (Report No. HB-83–630-EX). Groningen, The Netherlands: University of Groningen, Heymans Bulletins Psychological Institute.

MÜLLER, H. (1987). A Rasch model for continuous ratings. *Psychometrika, 52,* 165–181.
MURAKI, E. (1990). Fitting a polytomous item response model to Likert-type data. *Applied Psychological Measurement, 14,* 59–71.
MURAKI, E. (1992). A generalized partial credit model: Application of an EM algorithm. *Applied Psychological Measurement, 16,* 159–176.
MURAKI, E. (1993). Information functions of the generalized partial credit model. *Applied Psychological Measurement, 17,* 351–363.
MURAKI, E. (1997). A generalized partial credit model. In W. J. van der Linden & R. K. Hambleton (Eds.), *Handbook of modern item response theory* (pp. 153–164). New York: Springer.
MURAKI, E., & BOCK, R. D. (1999). *PARSCALE: IRT item analysis and test scoring for rating-scale data, Version 3.5.* Chicago: Scientific Software International.
MURAKI, E., & CARLSON, J. E. (1995). Full-information factor analysis for polytomous item responses. *Applied Psychological Measurement, 19,* 73–90.
NICHOLS, P. (1998, April). *Construct-centered framework for the conceptualization of measurement precision.* Paper presented at the annual meeting of the National Council on Measurement in Education, Session E1, San Diego.
OSTINI, R. (2001). *Identifying substantive measurement differences among a variety of polytomous IRT models.* Unpublished doctoral dissertation, University of Minnesota, Minneapolis.
RASCH, G. (1960). *Probabilistic models for some intelligence and attainment tests* (G. Leunbach, Trans.). Copenhagen: The Danish Institute for Educational Research.
RASCH, G. (1961). On general laws and the meaning of measurement in psychology. In *Proceedings of the Fourth Berkeley Symposium on Mathematical Statistics and Probability* (pp. 321–333). Berkeley: University of California Press.
RASCH, G. (1966). An individualistic approach to item analysis. In P. F. Lazarsfeld & N. W. Henry (Eds.), *Readings in mathematical social science* (pp. 89–107). Cambridge: MIT Press.
RASCH, G. (1977). On specific objectivity: An attempt at formalizing the request for generality and validity of scientific statements. *Danish Yearbook of Philosophy, 14,* 58–94.
REISER, M. (1981). Latent trait modeling of attitude items. In G. W. Bohrnstedt & E. F. Borgatta (Eds.), *Social measurement: Current issues* (pp. 117–144). Beverly Hills: CA: Sage.
RIMOLDI, H. J. A., & HORMAECHE, M. (1955). The law of comparative judgment in the successive intervals and graphic rating scale methods. *Psychometrika, 20,* 307–318.
ROGERS, H. J., & HATTIE, J. A. (1987). A Monte Carlo investigation of several person and item fit statistics for item response models. *Applied Psychological Measurement, 11,* 47–57.
ROSKAM, E. E. (1995). Graded responses and joining categories: A rejoinder to Andrich's "Models for measurement, precision, and the nondichotomization of graded responses." *Psychometrika, 60,* 27–35.
ROSKAM, E. E., & JANSEN, P. G. W. (1989). Conditions for Rasch-dichotomizability of the unidimensional polytomous Rasch model. *Psychometrika, 54,* 317–332.
ROST, J. (1988a). Measuring attitudes with a threshold model drawing on a traditional scaling concept. *Applied Psychological Measurement, 12,* 397–409.
ROST, J. (1988b). Rating scale analysis with latent class models. *Psychometrika, 53,* 327–348.
ROST, J. (1988c). Test theory with qualitative and quantitative latent variables. In R. Langeheine & J. Rost (Eds.), *Latent traits and latent class models* (pp. 147–171). New York: Plenum.
ROST, J. (1990). Rasch models in latent classes: An integration of two approaches to item analysis. *Applied Psychological Measurement, 14,* 271–282.
ROST, J. (1991). A logistic mixture distribution model for polychotomous item responses. *British Journal of Mathematical and Statistical Psychology, 44,* 75–92.

100

ROST, J., & von DAVIER, M. (1994). A conditional item-fit index for Rasch models. *Applied Psychological Measurement, 18,* 171–182.

SAMEJIMA, F. (1969). Estimation of latent ability using a response pattern of graded scores. *Psychometrika,* Monograph Supplement No. 17.

SAMEJIMA, F. (1972). A general model for free response data. *Psychometrika,* Monograph Supplement No. 18.

SAMEJIMA, F. (1973). Homogeneous case of the continuous response model. *Psychometrika, 38,* 203–219.

SAMEJIMA, F. (1975). Graded response model of the latent trait theory and tailored testing. In C. L. Clark (Ed.), *First conference on computerized adaptive testing* (pp. 5–17). Washington, DC: U.S. Civil Service Commission.

SAMEJIMA, F. (1977). A method of estimating item characteristic functions using the maximum likelihood estimate of ability. *Psychometrika, 42,* 163–191.

SAMEJIMA, F. (1979a). Constant information model on the dichotomous response level. In D. J. Weiss (Ed.), *The 1979 computerized adaptive testing conference* (pp. 145–165). Minneapolis: University of Minnesota Press.

SAMEJIMA, F. (1979b). *A new family of models for the multiple-choice item* (Research Report No. 79–4). Knoxville: University of Tennessee, Department of Psychology.

SAMEJIMA, F. (1983). *Information functions for the general model developed for differential strategies in cognitive processes* (ONR Technical Report No. 83–2). Knoxville: University of Tennessee Press.

SAMEJIMA, F. (1988). Comprehensive latent trait theory. *Behaviormetrika, 24,* 1–24.

SAMEJIMA, F. (1995). Acceleration model in the heterogeneous case of the general graded response model. *Psychometrika, 60,* 549–572.

SAMEJIMA, F. (1996). Evaluation of mathematical models for ordered polychotomous responses. *Behaviormetrika, 23,* 17–35.

SAMEJIMA, F. (1997a). Departure from normal assumptions: A promise for future psychometrics with substantive mathematical modeling. *Psychometrika, 62,* 471–493.

SAMEJIMA, F. (1997b). Graded response model. In W. J. van der Linden & R. K. Hambleton (Eds.), *Handbook of modern item response theory* (pp. 85–100). New York: Springer.

SAMEJIMA, F. (1998). Efficient nonparametric approaches for estimating the operating characteristics of discrete item responses. *Psychometrika, 63,* 111–130.

SCLOVE, S. L. (1987). Application of model-selection criteria to some problems in multivariate analysis. *Psychometrika, 52,* 333–343.

SMITH, R. M. (1987). Assessing partial knowledge in vocabulary. *Journal of Educational Measurement, 24,* 217–231.

SMITH, R. M. (2000). Fir analysis in latent trait measurement models. *Journal of Applied Measurement, 1,* 199–218.

SMITH, R. M., SCHUMACKER, R. E., & BUSH, M. J. (1998). Using item mean squares to evaluate fit to the Rasch model. *Journal of Outcome Measurement, 2,* 66–78.

SPEARMAN, C. (1904). The proof and measurement of association between two things. *American Journal of Psychology, 15,* 72–101.

SYMPSON, J. B. (1983, June). *A new item response theory model for calibrating multiple-choice items.* Paper presented at the annual meeting of the Psychometric Society, San Diego.

THISSEN, D. (1991). *MULTILOG, 6.0.* Chicago: Scientific Software Incorporated.

THISSEN, D., & STEINBERG, L. (1984). A response model for multiple choice items. *Psychometrika, 49,* 501–519.

THISSEN, D., & STEINBERG, L. (1986). A taxonomy of item response models. *Psychometrika, 51,* 567–577.

THISSEN, D., & STEINBERG, L. (1988). Data analysis using item response theory. *Psychological Bulletin, 104,* 385–395.

101

THISSEN, D., & STEINBERG, L. (1997). A response model for multiple-choice items. In W. J. van der Linden & R. K. Hambleton (Eds.), *Handbook of modern item response theory* (pp. 51–65). New York: Springer.

THISSEN, D., STEINBERG, L., & FITZPATRICK, A. R. (1989). Multiple-choice models: The distractors are also part of the item. *Journal of Educational Measurement, 26,* 161–176.

THORNDIKE, E. L. (1904). *An introduction to the theory of mental and social measurements.* New York: Science Press.

THURSTONE, L. L. (1925). A method of scaling psychological and educational tests. *Journal of Educational Psychology, 16,* 433–451.

THURSTONE, L. L. (1927a). A law of comparative judgment. *Psychological Review, 34,* 273–286.

THURSTONE, L. L. (1927b). A unit of mental measurement. *Psychological Review, 34,* 415–423.

THURSTONE, L. L. (1928a). An experimental study of nationality preferences. *Journal of General Psychology, 1,* 405–425.

THURSTONE, L. L. (1928b). A scale for measuring attitude toward the movies. *Journal of Educational Research, 22,* 89–94.

THURSTONE, L. L. (1929). Theory of attitude measurement. *Psychological Review, 36,* 222–241.

THURSTONE, L. L. (1931). The measurement of social attitudes. *Journal of Abnormal and Social Psychology, 26,* 249–269.

THURSTONE, L. L. (1937). Psychology as a quantitative rational science. *Science, 85*(2201), 227–232.

TUTZ, G. (1990). Sequential item response models with an ordered response. *British Journal of Mathematical and Statistical Psychology, 43,* 39–55.

TUTZ, G. (1997). Sequential models for ordered responses. In W. J. van der Linden & R. K. Hambleton (Eds.), *Handbook of modern item response theory* (pp. 139–152). New York: Springer.

van der LINDEN, W. J. (1994). Fundamental measurement and the fundamentals of Rasch measurement. In M. Wilson (Ed.), *Objective measurement: Theory into practice* (Vol. 2, pp. 3–24). Norwood, NJ: Ablex.

van ENGELENBURG, G. (1997). *On psychometric models for polytomous items with ordered categories within the framework of item response theory.* Unpublished doctoral dissertation, University of Amsterdam.

VERHELST, N. D., GLAS, C. A. W., & de VRIES, H. H. (1997). A steps model to analyze partial credit. In W. J. van der Linden & R. K. Hambleton (Eds.), *Handbook of modern item response theory* (pp. 123–138). New York: Springer.

VERHELST, N. D., & VERSTRALEN, H. H. F. M. (1997). *Modeling sums of binary responses by the partial credit model* (Measurement and Research Department Report No. 97–7). Cito, Arnhem, The Netherlands.

von DAVIER, M. (2000). *WINMIRA 2001 users manual.* Kiel, Germany: Institute for Science Education (IPN).

WAINER, H. (1982). Robust statistics: A survey and some prescriptions. In G. Keren (Ed.), *Statistical and methodological issues in psychology and social sciences research* (pp. 187–214). Hillsdale, NJ: Lawrence Erlbaum.

WAINER, H., & THISSEN, D. (1987). Estimating ability with the wrong model. *Journal of Educational Statistics, 12,* 339–368.

WEISS, D. J. (1983). Introduction. In D. J. Weiss (Ed.), *New horizons in testing: Latent trait test theory and computerized adaptive testing* (pp. 1–8). New York: Academic Press.

WEISS, D. J., & YOES, M. E. (1991). Item response theory. In R. K. Hambleton & J. Zaal (Eds.), *Advances in educational and psychological testing* (pp. 69-95). Boston: Kluwer.

WILSON, M. (1988). Detecting and interpreting local item dependence using a family of Rasch models. *Applied Psychological Measurement, 12,* 353–364.

WILSON, M. (1992). The ordered partition model: An extension of the partial credit model. *Applied Psychological Measurement, 16,* 309.

WILSON, M., & ADAMS, R. J. (1993). Marginal maximum likelihood estimation for the ordered partition model. *Journal of Educational Statistics, 18,* 69–90.

WILSON, M., & ADAMS, R. J. (1995). Rasch models for item bundles. *Psychometrika, 60,* 181–198.

WILSON, M., & MASTERS, G. N. (1993). The partial credit model and null categories. *Psychometrika, 58,* 87–99.

WRIGHT, B. D. (1997). A history of social science measurement. *Educational Measurement: Issues and Practice, 16*(4), 33–45, 52.

WRIGHT, B. D., & MASTERS, G. N. (1982). *Rating scale analysis.* Chicago: MESA.

WU, M. L. (1997). *The development and application of a fit test for use with marginal maximum likelihood estimation and generalised item response models.* Unpublished master's thesis, University of Melbourne, Australia.

YEN, W. M. (1981). Using simulation results to choose a latent trait model. *Applied Psychological Measurement, 5,* 245–262.

# INDEX

Note: Page numbers in *italics* indicate an illustration.

104

# ABOUT THE AUTHORS

**Remo Ostini** is a Lecturer at the University of Queensland in Brisbane, Australia. He received his PhD in Psychology from the University of Minnesota in 2001. His research interests include personality and attitude measurement, the psychology of morality, and applied ethics. He has published research in such journals as the *Journal of Medical Ethics* and *Addiction Research.*

**Michael L. Nering** is a Senior Psychometrician at Measured Progress, Inc., located in Dover, New Hampshire. He received his PhD in Psychology at the University of Minnesota in 1996. His research interests include person fit, computer-based assessments, equating, and item response theory. He has published research in such journals as *Applied Psychological Measurement* and *Measurement and Evaluation in Counseling and Development.*